Satan Speaks!

Satan Speaks!

Anton Szandor LaVey

Introduction by Blanche Barton
Foreword by Marilyn Manson

Feral House

Satan Speaks! ©1998 by Anton Szandor LaVey
Foreword ©1998 by Marilyn Manson
Introduction ©1998 by Blanche Barton

ISBN 0-922915-66-0

A Feral House Book

The Publisher wishes to thank Gregg Turkington for his astute assistance with the text, and Blanche Barton for everything.

Design by Linda Hayashi

10 9 8 7 6 5

CONTENTS

FOREWORD
MARILYN MANSON

ANTON LAVEY was the most righteous man I've ever known. He honored his immorality, and had more faith in his peculiar axioms than any armchair Christian vacantly reciting John 3:16 ever possessed. Yet, despite his cynicism and apocalyptic view of society, he often hoped for a better world, or at least one in which intelligence and creativity were applauded. I find more respect for humanity in his blackest humor than in the passionless zealotry that perpetuates all other conventional religions. Even if I had never agreed with a word he said, it would be irresponsible not to appreciate the sheer brilliance with which it was spoken—not to mention his having the balls to come out and speak it.

I've come to realize that the truth is most often unwanted or believed to be a lie. In a world so full of shit, Anton LaVey cut through it with the best of them.

Someone once asked me for the secret to my success. I answered that if they weren't smart enough to figure it out on their own, they didn't deserve to know; and if I told them, it wouldn't be a secret anymore. Fortunately for me and for all of us, Anton LaVey shared his magic, and I think it has made this wretched fucking planet a better place.

Thank you for your support and inspiration,

Marilyn Manson

Introduction
Blanche Barton

DR. Anton Szandor LaVey, founder of the Church of Satan and ideologue of modern Satanism, died October 29, 1997, while this book was being compiled. His unconventional life and vocations have been well-chronicled; the reader is urged to seek out *The Secret Life of a Satanist* or other biographical profiles on the Black Pope to see how his life as a concert oboist, gun-runner, carnival calliopist, circus lion trainer, hypnotist, ghostbuster, and crime photographer formed a diabolical alchemy within him that bubbled forth as the Satanic philosophy.

Anton LaVey released *The Satanic Bible* in 1969 and it has remained continuously in print since then, something of a record for an original paperback. That book contains the essence of what Dr. LaVey proposed as his new sinister religion. However, some of LaVey's advocates recommend that those who are curious about his writings begin their curriculum not with that basic primer, but with *The Devil's Notebook,* the collection of essays that was published previous to this one. Anyone reading the essays published in either that book or *Satan Speaks!* will glimpse a man of cutting wit, eclectic passions and an uncomfortably clear perception of mankind. Good writing paints a portrait of a man to the careful reader and the man portrayed in these essays was exactly as advertised—strong, talented, demanding, funny, opinionated, romantic, fiery, decisive in mind and movement.

One reason Anton LaVey has exerted the covert and overt influence on fashion, music, entertainment, politics, and other popular culture arenas that he has over the past decades is because of his honesty. Strange, perhaps even insulting, that the Devil's Ambassador on Earth should be considered "honest." Anton LaVey has many detractors who would itch to dispute that claim, especially those vermin who rush to discredit people after they're dead. But I maintain that he was at the core an honest, honorable man who devoted his life to exposing injustice and pomposity. He's worthy of the status of anti-hero many of his admirers have bestowed upon him.

Nothing irked LaVey more than self-righteous self-delusion—and he saw it everywhere. He mercilessly carved up sacred cows of all shade, maintaining that nothing gives a human a broader license to kill, maim, or destroy than a frothy illusion of righteous indignation. That was true during the Crusades and Inquisitions; it is still true in this age of PC hypersensitivity and winning through victimization. Through his works, he endeavored to shine a glaring light on aspects of everyday life that all of us might feel oppressed by but would never dare to challenge. The Devil is known for using his pitchfork to poke holes in overinflated taboos. In his own writings, if LaVey felt himself becoming too grandiose, he'd bring himself back down to reality with a chuckle. He didn't have to think about it; he just did it. Anton LaVey speaks to the Devil in all of us. One near-universal phrase he heard all his life was, "I've always felt that way myself but never knew anyone else did." He held sacred that which others scoffed at, and snickered at shopworn parlor tricks others revered as truth. He found beauty in misshapen freaks and was repelled by the ugliness advertisers try to pawn off as beauty. You'll find that constant perversity and satire in all the essays contained in this book.

And yet, Anton LaVey never claimed his writings were direct revelations from Satan; he never claimed to be Lucifer Incarnate. (He did die and was resurrected in 1995, but that's another story.) It would have been an easy pose to strike, and not entirely unbelievable. His looks and bearing certainly reflected the image of the Gentleman Downstairs. His ideas evolved from his enthusiasm for Satanic sympathizers and reprobates like George Bernard Shaw, John Milton, Goethe, Mark Twain, Jack London, Friedrich Nietzsche, Machiavelli, Rasputin, the Romantic and Decadent poets—peppered with a liberal dose of the Johnson, Smith & Co. Catalogue of Jokes, Tricks and Novelties. His sense of timing and drama, which he wound throughout his music, his magic and his life, was impeccable. LaVey's system of sorcery (and yes, he did very much believe in and practice sorcery) was so complex and subtle that it would take several lifetimes to fully explore.

Anton LaVey liked to say that if he didn't exist, someone would have to invent him. He experienced both the delights and the detriments associated with the job of being the Devil's Henchman. The High Priest resonated with the evil archetype so completely that he attracted delicious extremes into his life—undying love, fierce loyalty, unconscionable betrayal, supernatural strength, and intense jealousy. I gain satisfaction in knowing that his many detractors who try to attack the mundane details of his life will remain forever clueless as to Dr. LaVey's true complexity. Though he never pretended to be the Devil on Earth, he was as close as we are likely to see—even in his denial of that very identity. Preserver of forgotten pasts, singer of lost songs, lover of fallen women, advocate of fitting justice, dreamer of wicked futures—how could we conjure up a more rakish picture of the Dark One?

There was no room for survival after death in Anton LaVey's philosophy. We live; we entertain pompous illusions about ourselves; we die. Too bad. And yet, if we mesmerize, irritate, inspire, or terrorize enough people, our names will be remembered. Dr. Anton Szandor LaVey has earned that right.

THE GOD OF THE ASSHOLES

İt is believed, by empirical evidence, that many people who professed no belief in a deity when younger turn to "God" when they get old. Presumably, the closer they get to death, the greater their need for the comfort provided by religion.

Well, I guess I'm no exception to the rule. I seldom touch on theology. Apart from my *Satanic Bible,* I have left all discussion of gods and their creators to others to debate or exorcise, whatever be their requirements. Now, I must confess, I have found God; or rather I should say I have found a God. He (yes, he is usually male, and I'll tell you how I know) is not the kind of God I want to get to know. He is a total asshole.

Why do I say such things? Am I trying to show how blasphemous I can get, because it's expected of me? I can assure you; if I appear rude, it's because there truly is very little good I have to say about the God I have discovered.

We all know what an asshole is. If God isn't an asshole, he certainly acts like one. He's completely unjust, a shit disturber, impulsive, capricious and mercurial, irresponsible and unpredictable, a spoilsport, bad loser, child molester, and stoolie. He thrives on intrigue, scandal and gossip; likes to punish the just and reward the rotten. It's true: he loves the common man. The commoner, the better.

¶

If a common man does not believe in him, He makes a believer out of the simple soul by killing his little girl or placing him into a precarious situation whereby the poor guy must pray to Him. In short; God is just like real, unthinking, insensitive, avaricious and petty people.

Of course, God is a very Jungian construct. He was created by small men to serve their needs, according to their needs. Then, after the limited minds of millions of stupidos acknowledged Him, the goddamn dummies pretended it was the other way around. They insisted that God created man. They admitted that God created man in His own image, but could never extend the similarity beyond that. Not wanting to portray God as a monster, they presented Him as a patriarch in a long white robe with go-aheads and a long white beard. That way they could make a stern father figure out of him, to set an example for His children. If Daddy says it's okay to act like an unthinking asshole, then it behooves His followers to act accordingly. Thus given a green light, His minions are off and running.

The collective power of all the minds that accept the god of the assholes gives substance to such a divinity. It displays the power of magic. It is the collective will of millions of ten-watt humans. By their very faith, their God becomes a reality.

His minions are quite correct in many of their theological presumptions. Their God watches over them—at least as well as their own fuck-up natures can do. If the god they have created sometimes appears callous, so do they. That's why He can be excused so easily. After all, He's only human, and you know what assholes they can be! If something is "God's will," it's because He is willful. But like "pride," it comes in both real and false. There is a big difference between "will" and "wilful."

I said I'd tell you why God is usually masculine in form. It's because most of his creators were guys. Since he's been around so long, enough female assholes have appeared that He might occasionally take on a female form. Knowing what a welsher and double-crosser God can be, don't be surprised if He isn't a guy in drag. God,

2

like his disciples, likes to make promises he can't keep; getting human hope up, only to let it down. It's a nice trick to boost His ego. It's called "prayer."

If God is what I reckon Him to be, and Satan represents his antithesis, I'll place my faith in Satan. I have self-respect. Thus, I must have respect for the personification I select as a divinity. I cannot respect assholes. I don't quite know which is worse, an asshole or a fuck-up—a wise guy or a dumbbell. Being as how the popular God seems to possess the characteristics of both, I want no part of Him. I not only reject Him, but I despise Him. He is all that is mean and spiteful and petty. I would like to blow Him away. If I thought that by firing my .45 into the air I could exterminate Him, I would. There are two things wrong with that kind of tribunal. (1.) Knowing "God's will," the bullet would come down on some innocent kid. (2.) If I kill God, do I really want all the assholes of the world praying to Satan? Isn't He too good for them? Too reasonable? Too logical?

Satan may have always actually ruled the world, but He had to provide the self-righteous with a Goodguy Badge. The assholes, placing great store on fancy awards and titles, elevated themselves to Godhead status by proxy, but couldn't admit it. Perhaps Satan wants no part of such people either. He knows that when they make a mess of things, He's the one who has to clean it up.

TO:
ALL DOOMSAYERS,
HEAD-SHAKERS,
HAND-WRINGERS,
WORRYWARTS,
SATANOPHOBES,
IDENTITITTY CHRISTERS,
SURVIVOR COUNSELORS,
ACADEMIA NUTS, &
ASSORTED TREMBLERS

Your Apocalypse is here. It arrived right on schedule. Just the way you like it, pickle in the middle with the mustard on top. Credit me for the revolution, but credit yourselves for the forms that it has taken. I provided the reason and the rebellion. YOU supplied the incentive and weaponry.

When I began my New Epoch in 1966 (not to be confused with your latter-day chickenshit New Age), I thought I might be alone: a dreamer and speculator with a few agreeable cronies. I found out differently. Pretty soon, word got out. No admen, no public relations agents—slimy fame claimers to the contrary. Just supportive weirdoes in the right places who shared my views. Soon there were mimeographed broadsides available.

The next year, every time I conducted an "event," the media turned out in droves. A wedding, a baptism, a funeral—and nude altars too. Pretty soon the husband of one of my Witches Workshop students, columnist Merla Zellerbach, did something very special. His name was Fred Goerner and he had just authored a book called *The Search For Amelia Earhart.* Fred said I should write a bible, and he felt sure it would get published. "Wait a minute," I said. "I'm not a writer, never have been, and never have had any aspirations." "That's OK, don't worry about it," said Fred. "You can do it." He introduced me to his literary agent, Mike Hamilburg, who brought a man to see me. His name was Peter Mayer, a dynamic new editor at Avon Books. We talked a little, and Peter asked me, "How soon can you have it ready?" Like everything else in my life, this was sort of unexpected. I had never written a book before, let alone a bible. Especially under a deadline. "Just say it the way it is," insisted Peter. "It'll be fine."

And so I wrote. The rest is history. I thought that after being taken as entertainment value, my book would straighten a few things out concerning Satanism. It did, for some who read it. For others, it just went in one eye and out the other. But a couple of years later, someone paid me a great compliment. They said: "Anton's no fun any more."

Whenever I got on TV or the radio, I was given a few seconds to say what they desperately needed me for. Someone else who had lost 240 pounds of ugly fat got 20 minutes of air time. A woman who saw Jesus on a tortilla had even more time to recount her experience. If Satanism was so hot, why wasn't I able to talk about it? The media loved the *topic,* but they couldn't afford to air the *truth.*

I was like Santa Claus. Except that I delivered the presents *after* they selected and wrapped them. I started getting the feeling that maybe what I had to say was dangerous. After the unexpectedly blasphemous impact of *Rosemary's Baby,* Hollywood needed to provide an antidote. They bought an absurd story from a devout Catholic named Bill Blatty and turned it into a blockbuster. I was actually banned from the movie set. It laid the ground rules for diabolic possession. A homicide inspector named Dave Toschi told me, "I bet it's getting a lot of people back into church, Anton." It did more than that. It brought back that old-fashioned Satan—the kind that good church-going Christians needed.

Then came the rest of the delineators, the experts, the vanquishers of evil. The survivors, the abused, the breeders, the ex-High Priests, the cops for Christ—bullshit artists all. Where was Freudian wisdom when psychiatry like *Michelle Remembers* was validated by the media? A "Satanic survivor" could grunt out 15 belabored minutes of applauded testimony, while a real Satanist was lucky to be heard above two whole minutes of studio idiots gasping and jeering.

Now, in your End Times, you blame Death Metal and its influence on youth. You fret over the quality and content of their sounds. You demand warning labels on shrinkwrap. You silly mush-heads. YOU listened to the warnings and examples set forth by the Blattys, Pazders, Geraldos, Oprahs, Sally Jessies, Bob Larsons and their identity-starved stooges. I wanted to tell your children what was RIGHT about Satanism: encouraging sensuality with achievement, outrage with justice, nonconformity with wisdom. Instead, YOU provided media saturation informing them what "real" Satanists do, what kind of noises they make when possessed. YOU encouraged them to rebel by the aesthetic standards YOU provided, and still you grouse when they gravitate to Slayer, Ozzy, Electric Hellfire Club, Mercyful Fate, Deicide, Marilyn Manson, Acheron, Morbid Angel.

Do you know what? I think those bands are great. I would also like your kids to listen to Liszt, Borodin, Saint-Saens, Dvorak, Ketelbey, Wagner, Puccini, von Suppe, Rossini, Romberg, Kern, Friml, Al Jolson, Russ Columbo, Nelson Eddy, Nat "King" Cole, and the marches of John Philip Sousa. But you never gave me the time to explain THAT to them. As panderers, you were too busy crinkling the fat around your avaricious eyes and rubbing your money-grubbing hands and thinking of ratings. Or else, as audience, you were too dim-witted to think anyone on TV or mainstream print could be misleading you about Satanism. It runs YOUR life, so it must be OK for your children.

You hypocritical self-righteous fools. YOU made Death Metal and Satanic Metal bands what they are, by YOUR standards of blasphemy—but with significant modification. Now the performers and the audiences aren't shunning the idea of Satanism. They now greet each slavering monster as a friend. They raise their arms in Satanic salute. By whatever form their sounds take; the lyrics, barely understandable in their guttural roar, hurl all your warnings and admonitions back in your faces.

YOU set the disturbing aesthetic standards which concern you now. If something bold and new will emerge from it, it won't be to your credit. It will be because enough young people are seeing OTHER arenas of Satan. Your hysterical plan has backfired. YOU brought about your own Apocalypse, like the stupid masochistic victims that you are. You needed a Hell according to your own comfortable requirements. It didn't quite work out that way. Satan doesn't play by network, Marvel Universe, or Nintendo rules; or by Augustinian rules either. Soon your children will come walking in the front door with a *Satanic Bible* in one hand and a CD of Mussorgsky's *Night On Bald Mountain* in the other. Then, you'll know you're in real trouble. You wanted Hell. I'll give you Hell. It won't be fun. The Devil's Plan may not be your plan. Your Apocalypse is HERE. YOU brought it about. Take it. Suffer. It's all yours.

'T'ain't Funny, McGee

There is no sorcerer without a sense of humor. A sense of humor confers power in ways that cannot be learned. The following is the formula for a genuine sense of humor:

If you want to make your life easier, sometimes it helps to get a different perspective on things. Take seriously what others make fun of, and vice-versa. A true sense of humor is exhibited by this means. But first, it must be remembered that like intrinsic right and wrong, some things cannot be anything other than ludicrous. Others cannot and should not be funny. One who violates that basic rule is like a Christian "devil worshiper" who perversely tries to be "evil." At best, he is indiscriminate, and at worst, nurses a masochistic death wish.

Genuine misfortune appeals to the herd, who require to feel superior. The superior man sees comedy in that which others hold solemn, but is the misfortune of their own doing. Examples include impersonal tragedy, economic breakdown, and media-conditioned issues of all sort.

But it takes more than an ability to see the light side of serious things. One cannot have a true sense of humor without an equal sense of the profound. The familiar cliché of the clown whose heart is breaking holds great validity.

Invariably, those with the most finely-honed sense of humor find serious meaning in what everyone else ridicules. The very nature of the joke is its foundation of misfortune. The joke maker can spot the sham in acceptably serious situations. Then, having called attention to the deception, he may stand forth as a Satanic tribune. Not so easy is the reverse. The same rebel who defends the unpopular and the ridiculed, plays to an audience whose only illusion of strength lies in its ability to ridicule. It's interesting to observe how lower man, while realizing the sadness of clowns, seldom pays attention to them when they have serious thoughts to offer.

Some occupational and professional groups are conspicuously lacking in humor. At the top of the list are the occultists, who like counselors, lawyers, clergymen, social workers, interior decorators, fashion designers, and petty officials, lack any true professional purpose. The ranks of the most useless professions are always filled with the most humorless practitioners. A rule of thumb may be that sense of humor is in direct proportion to one's tangible worth as a productive creature.

How ironic, that occultists lead the pack of humorless persuasions. In their attempts to discover and utilize the arcane secrets of life and death, they fall short in the most important department. If seriousness is their stock in trade, many are born to the role. Like laugh tracks and applause signs, they flaunt their purpose—which is nothing. Occult studies is a haven for the impractical and inept, just as other useless tradesmen find asylum in other arenas. Were it not for his badge of office, the petty official could command no respect. Most social workers are only concerned about themselves, and sociologists don't laugh at dirty jokes—they just collect them. Of course, the reverse can hold true of sociologists; they enjoy the jokes so much, they become sociologists.

Psychiatry is often seen as a ghetto of marginal, run by deranged practitioners who are, in their own way, as nutty or nuttier than their patients. There is no profession that suffers the slings of lampoon as much as the most reputably serious. Death, being an exception to the humorlessness associated with it, entertains a larger than average number of humorously-inclined professionals. Perhaps that is why because of their proximity to death—those in the mortuary sciences often display a remarkable sense of humor. Unlike the occult arts, death is very real, very tangible, and necessary to deal with. There is little room for interpretation. Death is finite, discernible, and attendable. Its workers would go mad without a sense of humor.

Anyone who performs essential duties and leads an essential life has a higher sense of humor than pretentious-but-useless citizens. A strong need for identity precludes a sense of humor. One of the first refuges of the humorless is in the dismal world of comedy clubs. They remind me of a man I once knew—quite humorless—who was quick to identify a sense of humor as one who "laughs a lot." Like books on "How to be a Comedian," standup comics are among the world's most unfunny people. They don't have to be funny—their audience is usually comprised of similar drones. Its members "laugh a lot" because a professional comic—a specialist—stands before them and expertly says funny things, invariably on topics safely established as open to ridicule.

True humor is encouraged by individuality, rather than herd conformity. One must be removed from the contagion of established levity, the kissing cousin of the disease of false concern.

The Good Old Days:
A Devil's Advocacy

Having been a rebellious youth, I can attest that the "good old days" were not so good. First off, conformity—right or wrong—was king. Sure, we can talk about the parameters of conformity in today's world, and somehow equalize them with those of the past. It's easy to argue that one conforms just as much today, but to different standards. But I believe there is more room for individual, out-of-the-closet non-conformity than ever before—if the opportunity is taken. Things we now take for granted were once so tabooed as to be unthinkable.

In the good old days, if you didn't believe in God, you at least paid lip service to a benign supreme being. Oddly enough, the Devil did not constitute a threat and was able to be utilized in all manner of popular culture. He could appear in everything from food products to sports team mascots without consternation. As long as one believed in God, it was perfectly all right to entertain Satan for fun. If you were actually serious about metaphysical pursuits, you ran the risk of being pointed out as a strange cultist at best, or a devil worshiper at worst. The Rosicrucians were about as dark as you could get.

Institutions such as the military had no provision for alternative, offbeat religions. If you weren't of a Christian denomination, you must be Jewish—a separate kind of human being, tolerated at best. At least Jews could change their names and live like Christians and nobody'd be the wiser. Not so with people of color. They were stuck with their stigma. It is inconceivable today what real racism was like in the good old days.

Romantics like to talk of the slower pacing of yesterday. In many ways it wasn't so good. If you were traveling abroad and got homesick, you couldn't jump on a jet and be back in your own bed in a few hours. Mail was slow, and long distance telephone was a costly luxury. Well-made products were so well made that it took four strong men to move an item that could now be single-handedly lifted into a van (respectable folk didn't drive such vehicles for personal use). Backbreaking labor accompanied tasks that are now effortless. Driving a car was a greater risk. Tires blew out. Presumably efficient brakes failed. A slight nudge from a car in the next parking space was good for a cracked grill, dented fender, or locked bumpers. Radiators overheated and most vehicles, if subjected to today's driving conditions, would be stalled by the side of the road.

Clothing was of fine material—and heavy, uncomfortable, hot, scratchy, and hard to maintain. Creases were where they should have been, and kept that way, even if it meant not sitting down. Dress codes were rigorous. I could not buy a black shirt, and had to have them made. Beards of any sort were only worn by psychologists, stage magicians, old mariners, and Santa Claus. Adornments like earrings on a man were unknown. No respectable man had tattoos, and if a woman didn't wear a corset or girdle, she was a slut. Men's hair could be worn longer on top if it was whitewall on the sides and back—never long like a girl's.

Schools had truant officers and were run more strictly than prisons are now. They was no place for an unregimented child, no matter how brilliant. Today, a person can enjoy heavy metal and still listen to classical music. Yesterday, a kid was an "icky" or "longhair" if he preferred classical. Team sports were mandatory if you opted for peer acceptance. I wonder how many gun-toting marginal types got their start (as I did) protecting themselves from average kids?

If you were white, Christian, and liked sports, you were safe from criticism and considered All Right. It was truly the era of the WASP. All others were ghettoized—for their own peace of mind.

Sex was marvelously prurient—too much so, in some ways. Masturbation was a sin and a sickness, and sex before marriage disqualified anyone from public acceptance. Most marriages served a single purpose—to fuck and get fucked. When one considers the elaborate pageantry accompanying contractual vows, and for a single simple purpose, the guilts imposed by religion become glaring. Even more depressing to contemplate are the eugenic effects of entire societies born of such unions. It could be likened to the fates of entire nations determined by the regularity of their bowels.

Commerce in personal hygiene products had not yet become the supreme qualifier. But freedom from constipation had. If you were not "regular," you existed within a special purgatory, along with masturbators and eaters of garlic. Cleanliness was next to godliness—except privately. Generally, people smelled pretty strong. Heavier clothing made them sweat more, and normal activity was strenuous enough to work up a sweat. There are more things available now to reduce the danger of offending, but activity is less strenuous and less likely to work up a sweat. Exercise was what one got enough of at work. Women needed no workouts. Housework took care of that.

The language was without the sort of profanity expected today. Yet you could insult or offend with impunity. Profanity, like sex, was euphemized by terms which may have conveyed the message, but left much to be desired as catharsis. What one felt like saying was not what one actually said. Shoot!

"Understanding" was limited to learning, not human relations. Intolerance was rampant, because it gave the little man a chance to feel superior. Conformity was so important it made anyone who was slightly different fair game for ridicule or insult. There were no "special people." It was a much crueler world for the elderly, the handicapped, and children. Hypocrisy was everywhere because self-righteousness was easily maintained. Though standards in the arts were higher, respect was universal to questionable titles like "Reverend." A "prominent educator" covered a lot of undeserved ground. Any "college man" was prestigious enough to ensure respect, and armchair generals always had their share of wide-eyed disciples.

Wartime exploits were every man's claim to fame. Woe unto the fellow who had no buddy-time experiences to relate. You were expected to listen to an ex-serviceman's tales. Now, one can walk away with a clear conscience. The guy on the next barstool has no captive audience. Con artists and poseurs always had an audience because everyone was more polite and well-mannered and trusting to a fault. If you locked your door, you were either some kind of paranoid crackpot or else had something to hide. Because there were no "collectibles," nothing was worth hiding or locking up. Collectibles were thought of as "junk" to be thrown out. A car over five years old was a "jalopy" and not to be taken seriously, even though it may have been a custom Packard or Stutz. Older cars wound up appreciated by high school youths as canvasses upon which to paint inane slogans.

Books were treated as "friends" by scholars, but even scholars mistreated their friends miserably, using bacon for bookmarks. Magazines were handled like fish wrapping. Everyone was heavy-handed and heavy-footed. The exceptions were "artistic" types, considered prissy and effeminate. If you weren't "artistic," and wanted to be more than a churl—a "man in the street"—you had better be prepared to physically defend your sensibilities. Human interaction was more visceral (personal injury suits didn't yet abound) and one had to occasionally prove that he was not, indeed, a sissy. A kid could get beaten up for reading Plato or carrying a violin case (unless there was a machine gun inside).

"Gay" meant "happy and carefree." If you were homosexual, you were a pansy, queer, fruit, or all-around pervert. Again, with normal sex seeming prurient, hidden homosexuality was even more so. And the hypocrisy: the choir masters, scoutmasters, sports coaches, camp directors, gym teachers—and priests—all above and beyond reproach. Consequently, much more actual abuse occurred than today, when alternative sexual preferences don't have to be cloaked in sacrosanct credentials or rah-rah overcompensation. The irony is in the honesty and blasphemous openness once exhibited by flagrant homosexuals, who were invariably the most intellectually stimulating individuals in every crowd. Theirs was not a group identity, but a personal one, devoid of evangelism and conversion. They didn't care if the world turned gay, or even felt their influence. Now, the closet clerks and gymnasium gropers have healthier (and gayer) competition, without true deviance.

Food preferences were not catered to in the good old days. Anything other than "Amurican" had limited availability. Though maligned, fast food often has taste and becomes the easily obtained meal of choice. Pizza could only be eaten in an ethnic neighborhood, with perhaps only a single such specialty place serving an entire city. Likewise with Asian or Mexican food.

Despite complaints about the dearth of "good" music, listeners to the classics never had it so good. It's all there, if one wants it. An entire symphony may be purchased for a fraction of its 1940 price, and heard nonstop on cassette or CD. The same selection constituted 10 pounds of highly breakable records, with a change break every few minutes. An entire collection of favorite films can be owned and viewed by anyone with a VCR. In the past, only the very privileged could afford private projection facilities.

The list grows. Once, if you owned or rode a motorcycle, you were stigmatized as a wild nut. If you used a bicycle for transportation, and were over the age of 14, you were surely an eccentric given to a diet of nuts and berries, and garbed in baggy tweeds. If you didn't hunt for sport, you were a milksop sissy. Martial arts were known only as "jooey jitsoo" and practiced by sneaky yellow bellies. A real man put on the gloves and fought like a real man. If a young man didn't dance, he was a geek who could never expect to get a girl. If a young girl didn't cook and sew, no guy would ever marry her.

All kids wanted to play cowboys and Indians, themselves always being the cowboys. A heavy kid was called "fatso"; one with glasses, "four eyes." The ideal build for a boy was like something you'd see floating in a toilet bowl, with a face to match. If you were too tall and too thin, you were "death warmed over." Girls cursed with aquiline (big) noses, large feet, and over five-foot-four were considered ugly and avoided. A girl with glasses was destined to be a librarian and spinster, and presumed to be all dried up. Today's standard for female beauty is exactly what was then considered ungainly and homely.

Don't you wish you could go back to those days of yesteryear, when the greatest goal was to become President? Then, everyone would love and respect you.

THE TASMANIAN DEVIL

I learned a great lesson in self-awareness from a Tasmanian devil. Let me tell you how.

When I was in my teens, during my carny days, I knew an old showman named Ben Davenport. Ben was a master at presentation and ballyhoo rivaled only by Barnum himself. He bought an old genuine steam calliope and restored it as new, all white with gold trim. He displayed an oversized chimp as a rare and vicious Tasmanian gorilla who had killed his poor father after tearing his arm off.

Ben also had a Tasmanian devil, the first one I'd encountered. He had acquired the devil as a cub, through questionable sources, with the intention of raising it with as much love and care as was possible to give a Tasmanian devil. Then upon adulthood, presumably he would have an attraction as fierce as his Tasmanian gorilla.

He had correctly anticipated that the chimp, turned gorilla, would enjoy acting ferocious. Chimps are consummate actors and love to perform. And they *can* be mean, actually much more so than their supposedly savage gorilla relatives. A Tasmanian devil, figured Ben, was *naturally* truculent. All he'd have to do is stick the animal in a cage and let it, like a geek, act mad. But something went wrong.

First off, the devil did little more than sleep. When he awakened periodically he would attack the food Ben tossed into his cage, devouring it like most humans eat fast food. Then, after some snuffling around and a good deal of scratching himself, the devil would take another nap. It appeared that this devil had brought his Tasmanian fleas with him. Ben suspected that the devil might feel happier—but still mean—if he could be rid of his Tasmanian fleas. He tossed a pail full of flea dip on the animal one day, let it set for a while, then hosed the little fellow down. The devil, by this time named "Beelzebub"—"Bub" for short—went to sleep before he even dried off. Upon awakening, Bub attacked his dinner as usual.

A few days later a strange thing happened. Bub had finished eating, and was snuffling against the chain link of his cage, rubbing himself and eyeing Ben with what could be construed as affection. Making little grunting sounds, Bub acted almost as though he wanted to play. Ben tossed an old shoe into Bub's box, and before long, Bub was batting it around. Then Bub went to sleep—*with the shoe.*

Within two days, the devil was eating from Ben's hand, and gently. Bub still acted angry, however, when approaching the food in his cage, going through a sort of ritual of attacking it. After he completed his ritual, he'd eat like a cat, savoring each bite. It was then that Ben realized Tasmanian devils are fierce because they are in constant discomfort from Tasmanian fleas. Sleep provided protective pain relief. These could be the same fleas that made the nearly extinct Tasmanian wolf—the thylacine—so feared.

To make a long story short, Bub became a star performer—because of a strong pitch. Even though he made a devoted friend and companion of the night (he was nocturnal), he still attacked his food. He enjoyed being handled and played with, which didn't fit his expected image. And he still napped during the hours the show was open to the public. Ben had produced an overnight change which Lamarck would have cheered.

It wasn't until many years later that I realized the lesson to be learned from Beelzebub, the Tasmanian devil: I was very much the same! I was nocturnal, preferring to set my own hours and pace, but truculent over the fleas that infested my life in the form of human beings. Being able to sleep 'til rested and removing the personal Hell of Sartre's "other people" has had a pleasing and certainly tranquilizing effect on me.

Oh yes—I almost forgot the spiel that Ben had to employ while exhibiting the Tasmanian devil: "Step right up, folks, the big show's about to begin on the inside—the ferocious Tasmanian devil—the world's meanest creature, which will attack anything in its path! See for yourself what's left of his former keeper—just a chewed up shoe he kept as a souvenir! He's just about ready to wake up from his nap, and thank the Lord he sleeps when he does, or we'd all be in big trouble! See him when he wakes up and you'll know why they call him what they do! The animal without feelings for anything or anybody! They're so rare because they even eat their young! On the inside, folks, on the inside! I think I hear him stirring now! Just keep away from his cage when he wakes up is all I got to say! The Tasmanian devil! You'll have nightmares, but they'll be worth it! Hurry, hurry, hurry!"

A Plan

İndications are everywhere that we, as Satanists, have an affinity for certain elements of both Judaism (unrealized and unspoken) and Nazism (recognized and spoken)—presumably incompatible. Many factors are involved:

The aesthetic of Nazism is grounded in black. The medieval black magician, usually a Jew, practiced the "Black Arts." The new Satanic (conveniently described as "neo-Nazi") aesthetic is spearheaded by young people who favor black clothing, many of whom have partially Jewish backgrounds.

They are not "Jews," however. Most have never been inside a synagogue. Nor are they Holocaust aficionados.

Through the medium of rock and roll, all white kids have taken up, without realizing it, a black cultural identity, one otherwise alien to them. Blacks are where they are today because whitey *insisted* on being part black, no other reason. If there is a "White Power" movement today, it's because of things getting out of hand.

If being a Satanist means being rooted in Judeo/Nazism, kids who are on the outside looking in will find it attractive to the extent that they will forge a pedigree, if necessary.

Jaffe, in his book *The American Jews,* predicted that a new and vast mixed demographic of non-practicing and part-Jews would require new identities, but in another manner neither as Christians nor Jews, but as something else. Without realizing it, Jaffe was describing Satanism.

His grouping is the future of Satanism.

Satanism has become a gravitational force. We know that it doesn't matter what you were before. Once you discover your Satanic persona, that's it. You knew it was lurking inside you. You just couldn't quite conceptualize it.

There are many children of mixed black/white unions. The only way they can deal with it is through new common denominators that render established stigmas as inconsequential. That is an important word here, inconsequential. Before a new order can exist, the old order must be rendered inconsequential. Satanism has done that. Each year renders Christianity less of an enemy and more *inconsequential.*

Hereditary Jewish culture is a perfect springboard for anti-Christian sentiment. The Jews have a foot in the door as the only historically consistent scapegoated enemies of Christ. Despite some anti-Christians' (especially neo-Odinist and neo-pagan) claims that their abhorrence is based on Christianity's "Jewish origins," such a factor has not held much popular consideration over the centuries. Persecution of Jews occured largely because of "majority rules" populist concurrence that Jews killed Christ. Said to totally lack Christian values, Jews are therefore to be despised. When confronted with the notion that Jesus himself was a Jew, well ... he paid for his sin. Or as Marx (Groucho) would say, "We'll just pass over that." Funny thing—you don't hear many of the same observations about Torquemada. That's different.

To be a Satanist is, by association, already to be aligned with the universal devil Jew. The Jews have always had the Devil's name. They just haven't owned up to or taken pride in it, but rather have attempted to defend themselves against it. Instead of declaring that Jesus was a nut and a shit disturber and he got what he deserved and we'd do it all over again, they decided to infiltrate the Christian world and survive that way. For the first time in history, we, as a body of Satanists, have taken the Devil's name—and are proud of it.

The "new Jew," probably a mixture by birth, has no compunction about participating in the current avalanche of Satanic popularity. There is no longer a tendency to remain "good." That was for the old and humble Talmudic Jews who never wanted to rock the boat, and desperately tried to retain acceptance in a non-Jewish society. The day of the guilt-ridden Jewish liberal began to wane after the hippies vacated the premises. The only ones left seem to be among the yuppie-but-guilty affluent stragglers.

Just as the Nazis "Aryanized" certain needed Jews, we will see even more of the same phenomenon, given the pragmatically Jewish/Satanic connection. Gentiles without a drop of Jewish blood might concoct genealogical evidence of a Jewish great-grandfather, thus making them by heredity, generational Satanists. It could become even more desirable than having a great-great-grandmother who was burned at the stake as a witch. And why more desirable? Because Grandpa was a winner, Grandma was a loser. Grandpa may have been a Jew, but he was a survivor and maybe even made something special of himself, despite his devil's name. The burned grandmas, very few of whom were actually Jews, were "witches" for reasons other than their religious affiliations. If Jews were destroyed in wholesale lots, it wasn't because they were witches, but because they were Jews, whose only purpose in life was to kill Christians and propagate evil. The Isobel Gowdies may have been the condemned and executed witches, but the Jews were all devils.

It will become easier and more convincing for any Satanist to combine a Jewish lineage with a Nazi aesthetic, and with pride rather than with guilt and misgiving. The die is cast with the vast numbers of children of mixed Jewish/Gentile origins. They need a place to go. They need a tough identity. They won't find it in the Christian church, nor will they find it in the synagogue. They certainly won't find acceptance among identity anti-Christian anti-Semites who use noble, rich, and inspirational Norse mythology as an excuse and vehicle to rant about the "ZOG." The only place a rational amalgam of proud, admitted, Zionist Odinist Bolshevik Nazi Imperialist Socialist Fascism will be found—and championed—will be in the Church of Satan. Say! That's not a bad sounding name for something! "The Church of Satan!"

Entertain Me

What is there to see if I go outside? Don't tell me. I know. I can see other people. I don't want to see other people. They look awful. The men look like slobs and the women look like men. The men have mush faces framed by long hair and the women have big noses, big jaws, big heads, and stick-like bodies. That depresses me. It's no fun to people-watch anymore because there's so little variety in types.

You say it's good to get a change of scenery. What scenery? New buildings? New cars? New freeways? New shopping malls? Go to the woods or a park? I saw a tree once. The new ones look the same, which is fine. I even remember what the old ones look like. My memory isn't that short. But it's not worth going to see a squirrel grab a nut, or fish swimming around in a big tank if I must put up with the ugly contemporary human pollution that accompanies each excursion. The squirrel may enliven me and remind me of better vistas but the price in social interaction isn't worth it. If, on my way to visit the squirrel, I encounter a single person who gains stimulation by seeing me, I feel like I have given more than I've received and I get sore.

If every time I go somewhere to see a fish swimming, I become someone else's stimulation, I feel shortchanged. I'll buy my own fish and watch it swim. Then, I can watch the fish, the fish can watch me, we can be friends, and nobody else interferes with the interaction, like trying to hear what the fish and I are talking about. I won't have to get dressed a certain way to visit the fish. I needn't dress the way my pride dictates, because who's going to see me? I needn't wear any pants. The fish doesn't care. He doesn't read the tabloids. But, if I go out to see a fish other than my own, I'm right back where I started: entertaining others, which is more depleting than visiting the new fish is entertaining.

Maybe I should go to a coffee house. I find no stimulation in watching ordinary people trying to put the make on other uninteresting people. I can fix my own cup of coffee and not have to look at or talk to other people. No matter where I go, I stimulate others, and have been doing so all my life. It used to be I'd sometimes get stimulated back. If I looked up a pretty girl's dress, I might see dirty underpants. No more. If I turn on the radio, I can't hear Rudy Vallee, so forget it. I can't watch TV. It sucks out my brain. I see these poor slobs who are my age or older, and they are up on things I don't want to know about. The young ones don't know what I'm talking about—don't know about Jack, Doc, and Reggie; or Shostakovich's First Symphony. If I tell them, then I'm an unpaid teacher without tenure and it's a cinch they're not going to give me any credit. They're not even going to call a talk show and say, "I found out something from Anton LaVey that I think everyone should know about. Anton LaVey, of the Church of Satan, said that Scotty dogs were once popular because President Roosevelt had one, and the dog's name was Fala." The caller hadn't known that. Chances are good, the listeners didn't know that. Yet it's more valid information than some lousy creep's opinion about what we should do with repeat offenders in homosexual rape cases.

Of course, the answer to the aforementioned is that nobody really cares about Fala. OK. Fine. Then why should I care about them? They would be interested if I talked about Satanism, but then I'd be entertaining and stimulating and whatever they would pay me—which they wouldn't—would be insufficient to buy the kind of fish I'd be able to visit without my pants on, so why bother?

24

Acquisition

I often wonder if others who have acquired their material desires feel as I do. When I consider the parable and message imparted by "Rosebud" in *Citizen Kane,* I can identify with more than ever before. Now that I have many of the things I wanted, I lack the time to devote to them. Acquisition for the sake of acquisition has never appealed to me. I have never been a completist, nor have I set out to get anything I didn't want simply for the sake of eliciting envy from others. My power lies in other means.

So often I will dwell on the simplest thing. Fondling a beautiful little pair of jeweler's pliers can give me great pleasure—as if it were a priceless sapphire. It seems so clean, so free of taint, so devoid of the envies of others. A glass of clear, pure, icy cold spring water can become an ecstatic elixir, to be sipped and savored more than the finest vintage wine.

I own cars I do not drive, books I do not read, and friends I do not see, yet they are out there, and that serves my needs for them until a time I may want to partake of them. It's not that I don't cherish them, it's just that I am easily sidetracked by easy homage to an accessible thing and my indolence gives it priority. That's why I will read a conveniently-placed book over and over again. I never think, "Why do I spend so much time looking at this same lousy book, when I could select another from my library?" It's just that I'm actually *satisfied* to peruse the same book repeatedly. It does not pain or inconvenience me, but fills my time instead. Is that really any different than gazing into the same pool of water over and over again? One sounds so spiritual, while repeatedly reading the same catalog, to others, appears dull and pointless. To me, the principle is the same.

I acquire few new things, because I already have more than I can possibly attend to. Swords I do not polish, guns I do not shoot, cameras without film, telescopes without stars. In a world dependent upon consumerism, I am a burnout. I should want something new. Or at least improved. I don't. I am content to watch my son, my cats, my pictures on the wall, my cobwebs. If there is a need in my life for new and improved cobwebs, I have a deal with the spiders.

If someone told me I should get out and experience new things, expand my horizons, I could only ask, "Why?" I can go to the ocean and gaze at the horizon that's already there and not possibly desire anything better. If I want to experience new things, I can scrape a bit of paint from the wall, and observe what lies beneath. At the rate I am going, before long I may be able to understand the way of the monk, alone in his cell with his straw. I doubt if it will come to that, though. I love beauty and have known it. I will always need something I can hold in my hand that is well crafted and tactile. I will always need one of my past acquisitions, however inconsequential to others it may seem.

My acquisition of the moment is something I wanted, and obtained. It represents success, in a world of dissatisfaction and failure, anticipation and apprehension, striving, searching, hoping, struggling, scheming, swindling. The tiny object I hold in my hand is mine, but even more importantly: I am satisfied with it.

A Secret (Well, Sort Of)

The secret I'm about to reveal has served me well for most of my adult life. I realized its potency after I had unwittingly employed it.

It is based on a psychological principle that once a person has been brought to his knees, he or she will accept whatever master caused it.

It is the same principle which causes victims to become loyal to their abductors.

Most humans are masochistic, responding to fear and failure. That is a truth borne out by empirical evidence. Too many examples, over millennia, prove it beyond a shadow of a doubt.

The root of the word *subject* is the same as *subjective* and *subjugator.* Every monarch, every nation has its subjects.

I have observed that women are my strongest allies. It is not by accident, but by design. What I do not exercise to those ends by direct implementation, I do through my role with its fearsome and subjugating connotations.

If the public is a woman, a true leader must be a subjugator.

Carnal knowledge is one of the most primitive formulas for subjugation. It is the powerful subjugator for which women have had to employ mystery in order to combat. Carnal knowledge takes many forms, in many degrees. It is why I don't go about in t-shirts and bare feet. I will not cross over a line which makes me vulnerable. Only a pretty woman can expose herself for power, through vulnerability.

Rape fantasies in women who need them, are nothing more than one of many situations which fulfill woman's needs to be subjugated. Every woman wants love. Sex and love are so indelibly intertwined in woman, that by succumbing to a man of her choosing, however obtusely, she opens the portals of love.

It is not necessary to rape, assault or verbally abuse.

I make women wet their pants.

I give them an exercise in embarrassment. I allow them to break with convention, while experiencing subjective feelings of humiliation, shame, degradation, and, subjugation. But most importantly, release from responsibility.

I provide a return to earliest sexual awakenings, buried, but stronger in effect than any overt sexual possession. I assume carnal knowledge far beyond the pedestrian effects of rape.

I give back the father figure.

That is the Satanic.

Others have shared my secret. They shall remain nameless, though to divulge their identities would place me in the company of despots and tyrants, pop icons, legendary psychiatrists, and public figures beloved by millions.

The first exercise required by control groups like Scientology, EST, etc., is to be held captive in an audience which does not allow anyone to leave his or her seat. It is enforced—but voluntary—captivity. It also makes fanatically devoted followers.

My methods are far more honest, not resorting to transparent subterfuge akin to orgasmic holy-rolling in sin-killing tabernacles.

I explain plan, purpose, and method. No one is forced to participate.

If my own fetish produces dedication and loyalty by exploiting natural female requirements, no one loses. As for the tools of my trade and procedural details, that must remain a secret.

THE THIRD SIDE: THE UNCOMFORTABLE ALTERNATIVE

There are not always "two sides to every issue." That statement is a ridiculous slogan invoked by vested interests and perpetuated by minds of limited scope.

In matters of significant concern, there is invariably another alternative: a THIRD SIDE, a Satanic side.

"Two sides of the same coin" is what most major issues are artfully constructed to be. Subsequently, the populace lives by imperceptible Hobson's choices masquerading as opposing opinions.

The two uppermost points of the inverted pentagram of Satan represent the dualistic nature of all things, *as all things are naturally perceived.* Man has always been motivated and controlled by whatever dualistic concept is in fashion, and always will. Like it or not, it's the way things really are. Shades of gray only appear between *established* opposites.

The foundation, the spike, spur, piton and stanchion—the very strike of the lightning bolt of Satan—is the lower point of the pentagram driven into the ground. Not held aloft as a noble—but intrinsically useless—pointer toward heaven, but as a ground, or earth of wisdom for the horns above. Certainly, the lower point thrust downward implies the Trinity denied. Once that matter has been taken care of—and we *have* taken care of that—we must recognize the lower point of the pentagram for what it really is: the SWORD IN THE STONE.

The lower point *opened up* represents the opening of the gates of Hell, unleashing the Forces of Darkness into the upper world. That is why the founding body of the Church of Satan, the Order of the Trapezoid, originally employed that symbol. The Order of the Trapezoid is to this day the exclusive governing body of the Church of Satan, with its original symbol maintained as both a reminder and a sigil of enforcement.

The essence of Satanism is in the answers and solutions evoked by the THIRD SIDE—the lower point representing the sword plunged into the earth, the beard of wisdom seen on the goat within the inverted star.

It is invariably a third side that is overlooked in every issue and endeavor, from abortion to gun control. The third side can be the crackpot stuff of conspiracy theories, or it can be the most logical and simple, yet *deliberately neglected* conclusion.

For example, the science of eugenics provides *solutions* for the issue of abortion. Satanically speaking, I am against abortion. Yet I *do* consider a problem of overpopulation. Therefore, I advocate compulsory birth control. Unborn babies did not ask to be conceived. Once conceived, they should have loving, responsible parents, even if adoptive. A stupid, irresponsible woman should *not* have the right to "decide" what she does with her own body when in all other things, her mind is being controlled by impersonal vested interests. An unborn child's father should influence the outcome of a pregnancy if it can be determined that he is more responsible than the mother. If he is stupid, insensitive and irresponsible, he should be sterilized. Irresponsible parents, male or female, should simply be kept from conceiving children.

The most vocal anti-abortion crusaders are fundamentalist

Christians. Their entire plan and purpose originated with the same motivation that propagates any ethnic or religious grouping: to fill the world with more people like themselves. The women's movement favors abortion on the grounds that a woman's body is hers alone, to control as she chooses. Neither advocates mandatory birth control and selective sterilization, which—as a third side—could eliminate most of the entire issue. Of course, whenever an *issue* becomes more important than a *solution,* don't expect to stumble over a third side.

I respect someone who simply admits that he or she doesn't like kids—or dogs, cats, monkeys, zebras or potato bugs—for reasons of their *own.* It's when they cloak their reasons in the cant of populist causes, that I become truculent.

Other popular issues such as crime, substance abuse, and gun control have third sides which, if entertained at all, seem best left unspoken.

Satanism, which itself has become an issue, has a third side which exemplifies the message of what you are reading. The "two sides to every issue" scam purports that, to a fundamentalist Christian "expert," the threat of Satanism is a horrendous and engulfing amalgam of everything that is cruel, inhuman, sadistic, and monstrous. No reasons are presented other than a bid for power and a love of "evil." Conversely, the "other side" of the issue is presented by supposedly level-headed academic "experts" who, in their own threatened manner, minimize or dismiss Satanism as a trivial social aberration, practiced by a handful of insecure malcontents. The proponents of both sides have conveniently (and predictably) attempted to defuse real Satanism by inventing "different types" of Satanism, hopefully fostering the sort of sectarianism that undermines the solidarity of any potentially vast movement.

The third side of Satanism is, of course, the accurate, easily understood, and *truly* dangerous—to its detractors—side of Satanism.

Lest it be argued that the established Trinity has its place, the sigil of the Order of the Trapezoid must be knowledgeably viewed. As previously stated, the bottom point of the inverted pentagram corresponds to its anchor: Excalibur, the Spear of Destiny, Wotan's spear point, the lightning bolt that created the protoplasm of life as we know it. This central lowest point represents a rational resolution to the established but often extraneous opposing premises symbolized by the lateral two points. In the Order of the Trapezoid sigil these "two sides to every issue" only appear as reinforcing supports for the lowest point which, *opened up,* represents Hell Gate. Thrust upwards through this opening and into the central pentagon is the Devil's pitchfork or Poseidon's trident. This represents the pouring forth of the pure phlogiston from the deepest pit of Hell.

To the uninitiated, the Order of the Trapezoid symbol might resemble nothing so much as the fourble board of an oil drilling rig, with a pitchfork where the hoisted drill shaft would end. Or perhaps a railroad trestle or a squared-off suspension bridge. Symbolically and metaphorically, there is much room for speculation.

An actual Satanic "trinity" would be symbolized by an inverted three-pointed star of the configuration seen in the trademark of Mercedes Benz; or the insignia of the International Brigades, which fought in Spain in the 1930s as a test run for World War II. The sigil would then resemble the letter "Y".

Is it coincidence that the most important word to a Satanist is "Why?"

How To Be A Sorcerer

İn order to perform the supernatural, you must first be able to accomplish the supernormal.

In order to perform the supernormal, it helps if you are, yourself, supernormal. In order to be supernormal, it helps to be different. I mean *reallly* different.

That does *not* mean that you follow an established procedure or curriculum of esotericism, i.e. learn the fine points of occultic scholarship.

Can you honestly say that you don't know, nor care, what is happening in the news? Are you volitionally ignorant of popular culture—not up on any of the latest movies, performers, music, consumer products, etc.?

If the answer is "no," have you substituted recommended or prescribed alternatives—"cutting edge" interests and awarenesses?

How many people do you know who don't fall into either of those categories?

Isolation, exclusivity, and uniqueness are the first requirements of being "different" enough to be considered "supernormal."

A true sorcerer is never "up on things," because they hold no interest for him. Nor is he the least interested in "off the rack" esoteric and occult topics. He is an alien, and his pursuits and interests are virtually unlearned to those who know him. It's not that he takes any special pride in his alienation, nor does it worry him. He simply studies what he does and does what he does because it's the most natural thing for him to do. He is not "avoiding" anything to enhance his uniqueness. He's simply not interested.

One does not "evolve" or "become" a magician. There are no exercises, despite claims of esoteric orders. There is a cliche, "It's never too late to learn," which does *not* apply here. The special predispositions of someone different enough to be considered "supernormal" are cast at a very early age. Too much emphasis—for popular appeal—has been place on "hereditary" prowess. A tiny child in its formative years is a much more realistic candidate for later strange powers.

What's the upshot of all this? How does one learn? What exercises and measures can be taken to attain the status of the supernormal—let alone the supernatural? The answer? You can't. It's hopeless. Learn a trade. Develop a skill. Do at least one thing that sets you apart—like an extra tattoo on your little finger. Then, continue to "keep up with" the common denominators of your peers. You will still be full of magic—the magic of life that makes you move, act, respond, as an organism which needs no external wires. You are a self-contained miracle, as yet unreplicated. The independent scurrying of a newly-hatched spider or the shaky stumble of a newborn elephant may have an edge on you when it comes to the opportunity to become a real magician. But don't give up. You can become more magical than you already are. You can develop greater balance and equilibrium, without gyroscopes. You can learn to write (with a spell-checker), sing (with Karaoke), play (with a sequencer), and perform all manner of skills. But you will never be supernormal, supernatural, or a miracle worker. If it's any consolation though, you *are* a miracle, just the way you are. Almost as much as the much smaller spider or much bigger elephant.

On Women
or Why My Right-Hand Man Must Be A Woman

Please don't think I'm some kind of sex fiend because I prefer to talk to the ladies rather than the gentlemen. In fact, the prettier a woman is, the more I prefer her company. This sets me apart from those lavender limp wristed fellows who love the old biddies as well as the young ones and who used to frequent tea parties. Unlike them, I could never be a hairdresser. And I can't gossip well, which the beauty salon demands. Instead, I like to teach. My best students have always been women. They want to learn, rather than challenge. A male deficit is the need to lock horns. If a male is a she-male, it's even worse because a covert sexual agenda is ever present—one which I can never reciprocate. Hence, unless a man is eclectic, dignified, extremely capable, and gracious, I'm not really interested in maintaining a friendship. In a way, that is a great compliment to my male friends and close associates. A man must be superior, while a woman may be quite flawed, but blessed with enough in the looks and attentiveness department to get by.

I believe that woman is the dominant sex, with or without feminist validation. The main difference between liberated and non-liberated women is that liberated women are enslaved by homosexual men and women much more destructively than they would ever allow themselves to be by straight men. They are thrown off guard by self-serving cockless cunt cant. Then, disenfranchised of their natural

35

weaponry, they must compete with both gay and straight men, while relying on "new and improved" male weaponry. More often than not, they lose. Then, they wonder what they lacked and wander back to school to find out. By that time, they are certain they have lost the best years of their lives, and make even bigger fools of themselves desperately trying to make up for lost time. In order to improve their minds, they enroll in all manner of classes and courses conducted by fags and feminists, going from the frying pan into the fire.

Subsequently, the poor dears have been so thoroughly confused and demoralized that at the decrepit age of 35 they have forgotten, if indeed they ever knew, what it was like to be a real woman. If by some baleful fate, they should cross my path, and I should make the mistake of telling them how good they'd look in red lipstick, a dress, and high heels—they react as though there's something wrong with me. How dare I suggest that they reclaim their gender! Yet they appear to enjoy my time, even my attention—presumably as one guy to another. I must appreciate them for themselves—which adds up to an ersatz man at worst and an incomplete woman at best. No, thank you very much.

Getting back to my preference for the company of genuine, visually stimulating, gender affirming women: I believe that most heterosexual males would share my choice of companionship if given the opportunity. Many young males crave to be rock stars so they can have all the girls they want, screaming hysterically whilst climbing on-stage and tearing their clothes off. I find it ironic that these same young men are offended if I reject their petitions to meet with me, rob me of valuable time, and even apprentice under me; yet if the tables were turned they would reject my company in a moment given the option of a pretty girl to spend time with. The reason any man would prefer the company of other males is because he doesn't feel comfortable with women (including occupational demands), can't get a woman, or seeks approval from other men for whatever purposes are required.

İꞃ Pꞃaise Of Sycophaꞃts

I'm a sycophant. Also adulatory. If I admire someone, I can say so and give the reasons why. In fact if I like someone enough, I can not only speak well of them, but maybe even write about them. And they don't even have to be dead. As a matter of fact, it might be said that I am sycophantic about anybody I like. This is in line with my definition of Good and Evil: "Good is what you like and Evil is what you don't like."

Could it be that those who throw the word "sycophant" about in a pejorative manner, are so filled with self-loathing that they mustn't like anything or anyone for very long? There is so much "evil" in their small lives that the only reason they keep on living is to make trouble for others.

If I am bitter it's because I'm dismayed. Dismayed by mankind's need for strife and turmoil. Dismayed because man is nature's most imperfect (incomplete) creation and I must share his form. Bitter as I may be, I don't wish to be unhappy. Though I am bitter, I am not small and mean. I can praise. I can compliment. I can encourage. I can voice respect without the need to add qualifiers in the next breath.

Perhaps that is why I like sycophants. They enrich, enliven and encourage me. I started the Church of Satan because I wanted to indulge myself the rare privilege of hearing my own heretical views echoed back to me. No debate. No contradiction. No need to convert. Adversity may be strengthening but agreement is inspirational. What

37

good is strength if it only serves others' demands and expectations? "Constructive criticism" is only as sound as the status of its advisor. Consider the source of any suggestion. Is his expertise paying off? If so, at whose expense? Who is footing the bills for an advisor's exalted position? Do you honestly believe that you require counsel in matters you are equally, if not more capable of resolving yourself? If you had moral support—a green light—would that not be better than the obtuse advice of someone else? That's when and where sycophants come in handy. They're like a crystal ball, which, because of its tranquilizing and reflective nature, can free your mind for answers and inspiration.

Sycophants want to please you. If they displease you, they will vacate the scene, unlike others who thrive on conflict and stick like glue whether you want them or not. Sycophants are seldom masochistic, not wishing to incur your wrath. If they admire you, they want you to like them too.

Sycophants are led to believe that they are weak and impressionable, largely because they undermine a celebrity's detractors and critics. It is hoped that if a sycophant is made to feel lowly, he or she will withdraw support of the object of their esteem. Actually it is the sycophant who is strong and his detractor who is insecure and weak. It takes a sound ego to praise and respect another. Even more, it takes discrimination to know and praise another who deserves it. Not all sycophants may be discriminating in their choice of idols, but a sycophant's detractors seldom recognize *anything* of value. They are too tormented by the pain of their own insignificance.

I have made a rule that I will not meet with or entertain anyone who petitions me without their having advanced some respect or praise for me or my work. If asked, "Does someone have to agree with you in order to be your friend?" my answer is a resounding "YES!" My reason is that there are so many people who disagree with me and resent me, that I can use all the support I can get. Anybody doesn't like me or the way I do things can go fuck themselves. They are *not* entitled to their own opinion.

THE COMMON GOOD

NOTHING is done in the interest of welfare for the common good where there is money to be made. If charity begins in the home, someone is going to create a state by which each home is a cell, to be employed for the collective benefit of astute vested interests.

For example: there are no more quarantine laws for immigrants into the United States. Routes of contagion exist primarily through human contact. No winds need bear them any longer. Airline travel has done the job well. Intercontinental flights have provided a means of viral contagion unconfined to the plague sites of antiquity. Where immigrants once arrived penniless and in the steerage of ships, travelers of all purpose now arrive with slim cards of plastic and clothes that travel well, albeit as containers for diseased bodies.

No attempt is made to deter or detain the new plague carriers, unless it is suspected that they may be trafficking in illegal drugs or harboring small animals, bombs, firearms, or fruit flies.

Yet, most transmittable diseases—contemporary plagues which cause more suffering and death than all terrorist infernal devices and narcotics combined—are allowed complete freedom of movement. No one is detained by airport security or customs because of runny nose or suspected scratchy throat.

Airlines are in business to make money. Any multi-billion dollar legitimate business is going to encourage more of the same. Special holiday travel rates are presented as caring emoluments to a deserving customer. In fact, every seemingly generous dividend presented by any business is for the good of the business, not the customer. The dictum, "Americans love economy and will pay anything to get it" has been the bedrock of every special offer, sale, lottery or otherwise that preys upon guilt-ridden humans who want to steal something and get away with it.

Can corporate interests be blamed for maintaining a climate of unbridled greed and avariciousness in the name of benevolence? After all, does not the "common man" need to believe that *somebody* cares about his welfare? Does not the prostitute's john want to believe that his looks and personal magnetism are determining factors in his liaison—that ideally he consorts with his "girlfriend"? If businesses ceased to "care" about their customers, could they continue to exist?

As long as insecure and insignificant men and women's ego needs must be served—nay, *prioritized*—there will always be gratification in the form of some charity or welfare. Given that brutal premise, are not most herd human animals welfare recipients to a discernible degree?

If merchants really concerned themselves for the welfare of others, they would close their doors during the Christmas holiday season, thereby contributing to the peace and tranquillity that should accompany a time of the year when *every other living creature is either hibernating or dormant.* I would like to believe we have evolved to an extent that we no longer think the sun is dying, and that we must have a final forced fling of merriment before the world ends.

Sleepers, Orphans, and Scarcity

When "classic" is mentioned, it usually refers to and is synonymous with scarcity. A 1956 Ford is a "classic" on the grounds that there simply are not many on the streets. Those which are seen have been preserved or lovingly restored. No one ever threw them away or laughed at them or made fun of those who drove them. They were always "safe" cars to own and drive. Now they are "classics."

Then there were the "orphan" makes: the Nashes, Hudsons, Packards, Grahams, Studebakers. They were driven by non-conformists. They cost no more than the Big Three (General Motors, Chrysler, Ford) but were intimidating. Owners of the popular makes would never admit they were afraid to be different, hence their avoidance of those makes. The excuse was always, "What are ya gonna do when you need parts or repairs?" not realizing that there is a price to pay for individuality. It was an instant badge of non-conformity: "He drives a Studebaker…" Consequently, all the "orphan" make cars ended up at the back of used car lots for ridiculously low prices. They became the white elephants of the automobile world.

With the passage of time, those oddball cars were junked. Nobody saved them. Many were purchased in the first place because they were so cheap and, even if in excellent condition, were driven into the ground and then scrapped. They became scarcer than ever. The

Satanic irony is that now they are worth more. By their scarcity, they have become more desirable as collector's cars than they ever were before, even when new.

Everyone saved *National Geographic* magazines, with *Life* a close second.

It has been said that the Earth has been thrown a few degrees off its axis due to the weight of all the *National Geographics* that people saved. Of course, mothers threw out comic books when their sons grew up and moved out. Wartime paper drives claimed millions of magazines that were not considered worth saving. Now those comic books are worth thousands of dollars. As might be expected, an old *Look* magazine is scarcer and more valuable than *Life*. The same goes for the *Life* imitators: *Pic, Click, Vue, Parade, Peek,* etc. The reason: The imitators were not considered worth saving.

The list of examples is endless. A *Horror Stories* pulp magazine is much harder to come by than an issue of *Weird Tales,* and brings a higher price. The most cheaply made old toys are now scarcer and more costly than many more "showy" playthings of the same vintage. The inexpensive toys were expendable—played with until broken and then discarded.

Depression-era glassware and Dish Night giveaways are more sought after than Wedgwood china, and a nightstand-sized plastic radio brings more than an elaborate Hi-Fi system. A Victorian house is more saleable than a split-level from the '60s, and not because of its craftsmanship. It's because most Victorian houses were demolished as worthless, so there are fewer of them—and they are now associated with the gothic, which is quite saleable.

In a Satanic sense, that which is most unpopular is certain to become most desirable. Time is important; chronology is not. Even a broken clock is accurate at least twice a day. So, save your broken clock. The time on its face, however you set it, should let you know when to polish your shoes. If you don't wear shoes; brush your teeth. If you have no teeth have sex with a senior citizen, because there's many a good ride in an old Packard.

CHILD ABUSE

Every time parents visit their own needs upon children, they practice a tragic kind of child abuse. Solipsism, Satanic sin that it is, is employed by adults toward young children who willingly and enthusiastically accept their elders' guidance.

Parents raise their children according to their own requirements. It is they who need friends to palaver with, not their children. Therefore, "all children need playmates." Despite all evidence that insularized children are most likely to become prodigious, the pedagogy of parents dictates otherwise! Better to raise a dull, stupid child (just like its parents) than an unorthodox, but smart one.

"All children need sunshine," or so their cosmetically tanned parents dictate. Helpless babies are therefore subjected to the glare and radiation of daylight. If they are uncomfortable in the hot sun, it matters not. If their parents love it, infants must love it too—or else.

"Participation in sports teaches fair play and encourages healthy competition." What a laugh that one is, except to parents who need sports for stimulation and vicarious identification. And as for "healthy competition," sufficient incentive to excel could easily be provided by example—without the depleting stress of competition. When it comes to building good character, penitentiaries are filled with good folks who were raised on good sportsmanship and old-time religion. The only thing sports confers is a lasting justification for contentiousness.

Passing tests is finally being considered an invalid measure of real intelligence. Most schooling, as well as other human endeavors, demands that one of inferior station prove oneself to another, who by his position of authority (as tester) is presumed worthy. The trauma that tests can present to genuinely brilliant children is more than compensated for by the well-educated morons who become the "experts" in all fields.

Good Sportsmanship

What is "good sportsmanship?" Is not the term an oxymoron? Is not any sporting activity a polite justification for combat? If man ceased to prey upon each other, could he continue to exist?

If "sports" is a natural human activity to keep alive and hone the skills of self-preservation—the highest law—is it necessary to "civilize" it by shaking hands before and after each conflict? Has pretending to forgive one's adversary really helped to civilize mankind? Or has it actually stifled the resolution of change and progress, thus perpetuating historically observable stagnation?

If there are no victors, there can be no change; victory is the vehicle which overturns (or *should*) worn-out systems and ideals. To forgive the enemy is the Christian ideal itself. But by that standard of "good sportsmanship," isn't any productive purpose in combat or conflict negated?

I give you good sportsmanship: Two homosexuals—both masochists—are standing on a corner talking. One is relating the events of the past evening. He appears battered and bruised, with one arm in a cast and sling. He describes to his friend how he accompanied a newfound acquaintance, to his apartment. The apartment just happens to overlook the corner on which they are chatting. The injured dear proceeds to go into great detail over the indignities, both moral and anal, that he suffered. To climax the evening, he relates how his erstwhile partner physically threw him out the second-story window, thus ending the abusive and degrading encounter. That is how his arm was broken. As he is finishing his tale, the victim's frightened and darting eyes spot the man from the previous night standing in his window. He has been observing the friendly encounter from his apartment. Tapping his acquaintance on the shoulder, the battered fellow exclaims: "Oh ... OH! ... There he is NOW! Right up there in the window, watching us!" He proceeds to wave excitedly: "HI! ... HI! ... I'M NOT MAD!" So much for "good sportsmanship."

The great Ty Cobb has survived in baseball history as a villain because he treated his opponents badly. Perhaps Ty Cobb was the only real baseball hero who practiced true sportsmanship, rather than "good" sportsmanship. He disdained and discarded the niceties of ass-patting, hugging, squeezing, and other such lovebird waltzings-around. He rejected any notions of "beloved enemy" and "it doesn't matter whether you win or lose, just that you play the game." He was what a gladiator should be.

The asinine notion that the enemy must be allowed to lose with dignity is a Christian trait which reveals a masochistic need for the frustration of unresolved conflict. A defeated enemy should limp away, nursing his wounds, rubbing his lumps, and beaten in spirit. Then, though he sustains a grudge, he will think twice before he engages the same adversary for a return match.

If pride is a Satanic virtue, a Satanist goes only where his pride might prevail. If he wants always to walk away from a situation with his pride intact, he refrains from entering an arena he should know to be demoralizing. Jurisprudence and a strong awareness of his balance factor should dictate his assertive endeavors. In that way, he will know how to play the game to win, not to joust. And the decision his victory has effected will bring others to believe in what he believes.

CHOOSE YOUR WEAPONS

Very little has been studied concerning choice of firearms when dealing with homicide investigation. A great deal can be discerned about the type and MO of a killer by his weapon preference. Certain suspects can almost be ruled out simply on the strength of the incongruity of firearm and perpetrator. For example: a youth heavily influenced by pop culture gang violence is more likely to employ a "nine" (nine millimeter, large magazine capacity, semi-automatic) than a Colt frontier model revolver. Here are some guns and the folks who are likely to match them:

.22 caliber long rifle. This is an ubiquitous bullet used in everything from tiny derringers to mini spray-type assault rifles. Therefore it will be employed by someone whose prime concern is not getting caught. Because there are so many .22 caliber guns, there are even greater quantities of shells to go with them. Lots of practice is feasible because of cheap ammo cost. The guns themselves are among the best bargains, and therefore easily discardable without replacement worries. The weapons are, though smaller, less dear to their users, unless uniqueness enters the picture. Example: a fellow who uses a Whitney Wolverine isn't likely to drop it in the bay after doing his thing. Still a .22, it is difficult to identify, much less trace to its owner—unless a suspect turns up with a Whitney Wolverine. The Manson killings showed that Tex Watson had used a High Standard "Longhorn"—not a common gun. If the bent and rusty .22 caliber weapon had not been found by the side of a road and brought to the attention of authorities, they still might not know certain details, much less who they were seeking. The easily obtainable, easily disposable .22 is the first choice of professionals, who don't underestimate the lethal ability of the .22 slug. There are still more people killed by .22s than any other bullet, so the perpetrator could be anyone from a yokel farm boy to a contract killer.

.25 caliber ACP. This was a favorite in the '20s and '30s because lighter gun laws encouraged any "automatic" that could be carried in pocket or purse. Anyone (usually gun shop commandos) who says you can't do any damage with a tiny .25 auto is full of shit. Pick up any true detective magazine from the period and you'll see how many murder and homicide cases were played out by these "impotent" little "toys." Like cigarette cases and holders, the .25 appealed to sophistication. It was considered urbane to carry a .25 caliber auto, and there were lots of brand names, mostly variants of the baby Browning design. Now, a killer who uses a .25 must be either a kid who got it cheap, someone who doesn't like guns and feels such a little thing is less dangerous to have around, or a rare romantic who finds aesthetics and concealability a factor. The last type does not set out to kill, but happens to have the weapon on him when a provoked homicide is inevitable.

.32 caliber, .32 ACP or 7.65mm. This is the guy to watch out for—often the real nut who doesn't read the latest reviews in gun magazines. His gun is a highly personal companion with a "story" attached to it. He knows what damage a dedicated .32 can do and sometimes does it. At one time, standard police and service revolvers all over the world were this caliber. Millions have been killed by it. Then, after WWII, Americans decided that the size was inadequate and, like the automobile horsepower race, the caliber fell victim to "bigger is better." Occasional oddballs stuck by their .32s. The perpetrator who uses a .32 is more likely to actually kill than perhaps any other type, and executes his victim with almost clinical dispatch. A wise casting example of the type was played by Charles Bronson in *Death Wish,* wherein the weapon was a gift to an otherwise mild-mannered guy who had a purpose and used his new friend (the gun) as a vehicle to attain it. Since this weapon is now quite unpopular, yet highly personal, it can be easily linked to its user. Thus, he isn't likely to leave it lying around or toss it out the car window.

.380 or 9mm short. A sensible choice for the potential, if not actual, killer. Easily concealable, often double action (safe), it enjoys peer acceptance. The macho fellows at the gun show might glance at each other when they hear you speak of your .25 or .32, but will never bat an eye if you refer to your .380. The current personal protection pocket auto for knowledgeable practical people, but seldom used by killers.

9mm. The current weapon of choice, largely because of positive double action and large magazine capacity. Classic examples are aesthetically superb, but often lack double action and/or high cartridge capacity: the Luger (single action, limited cartridge capacity), Browning Hi-Power (single action), Walther P-38 (limited capacity), etc. Popular choices are owned by the most vociferous would-be killers—who probably would never do the deed. The occasional headline-making mass killer fires up the vicarious and copy-cats. TV shootouts spark pop appeal. This is not to imply the Glock, Sig, Beretta, Ruger and S&W "double nines" are not ideal working guns, but to caution law enforcement against assuming every killer wants and uses the same kind of military-level firepower they do (and this has become the most popular law enforcement weapon). One thing stands out: the perpetrator who employs this gun often looks the part, i.e., everything but the cammies.

.38 ACP. A bigger version of the .32 ACP, employed by a similar kind of oddball, but who demands more firepower and isn't caught up in the 9 mm sweepstakes.

.38 special. The most popular "wheelgun" five or six shot revolver. Almost like the .22 insofar as traceability; no souvenir empty cartridge cases left lying around. Cheap, easily obtained ammo. A good all-around sensible murder weapon. Because of Freudian upgrading, the .357 magnum may be even more popular for hot dogs, but like the Dirty Harry .44 magnum, is more for talkers than doers.

.45 ACP. The classic "I won't take any shit from anyone" pistola. Perps are chiefly concerned with blowing their victim away, rather than shootouts. Once the standby of ex-soldiers turned peacetime killers, this caliber intimidates as much as it kills. A traditionalist's weapon now used by "last straw" avengers. Even Wilhelm Reich packed one around during his final days. Perpetrators want to make sure their victims know they're up against serious business and give them something to think about while staring at that big hole in the front of the gun.

THE WITCH'S SHOE
AS WEAPONRY

The witch's spike-heeled shoe, while traditionally associated with easy virtue and availability, has been transformed into a symbol of womanly power. While still maintaining its allure and aesthetic appeal, its very design can transform it from a device for enticement to a deadly weapon.

By itself, with no modification, a stiletto-heeled shoe makes a formidable weapon. Available in an instant, it can be firmly grasped and employed to scrape, gouge, rake, and generally wreak mayhem on any pest who accelerates into assaultive status.

Body areas to go for are identical to those fully described in many competent textbooks, especially those dealing with pressure and puncture points most effectively attacked by edged weapons. Sources such as Loompanics can provide an arsenal of already published information.

At first thought, it would seem better to remove both shoes in a critical situation, for more efficient body balance and decisive movement. If you opt for that technique, wear "Ped" type liners inside your shoes, so your feet will have rudimentary protection from rough surfaces when your shoes are removed. Callused soles will serve as well.

If many witches spent more time callusing their soles and less time pumping iron and working out, they'd be better off in an immediate survival situation, while maintaining the graceful and voluptuous flesh of a compleat succubus.

The alternative to removing both shoes has its own advantages. The "one shoe on, one shoe off" technique consists of one shoe used as a hand weapon, while the other remains on the foot for kicking, scraping, and stomping your opponent. A stiletto heel ground into the top of your victim's foot can have a discouraging effect. If your hand-held shoe succeeds in doubling up your opponent, a pointed toe to the face, head, or groin can be struck with greater force from the leg muscles. You might consider steel toe inserts.

Velcro allows for unlimited resourcefulness in modifying witch shoes for combat. The sexiest and most dainty ankle strap pumps can retain their small buckles for appearance's sake, yet actually be secured against accidentally falling off by Velcro. A spike heel can be drilled out, creating a sheath or scabbard for an ice pick or dagger affixed to the shoe, which then serves as a substantial handle. The steel shaft fitted into its high heel sheath insures rigidity, while Velcro applied to the juncture of shoe and sheath/heel ensures permanence until the sheath/heel is firmly pulled off. A variation of the same modification is to keep the entire shoe and heel intact, drill out the heel from where it makes contact with the ground, and insert an ice pick with a tiny heel for a handle. Prophetically, many spike or stiletto-heeled women's shoes are constructed in this manner—a metal shaft being embedded into the heel for reinforcement.

For the more serious-minded Satanic witch, skilled in craftsmanship—or if not, with a friend who is—a spike heel makes an excellent holster. Instantaneously pulled away, it can reveal a substantially held pistol. Ideally suited for the job is the North American Arms five shot mini-revolver, obtainable in varying barrel lengths and calibers from .22 short to .22 magnum. Any derringer-type pistol will work admirably, with increased accuracy due to the extra grip provided by the body of the shoe. If questioned, the wearer can employ the old stage magician's technique of substitution, offering up for inspection the innocent shoe and allowing the Law of Invisibility to cloud the existence of the lethal one. This may necessitate pulling a switcheroo, temporarily replacing the right shoe on the left foot. Even the most astute observer will seldom notice whether a singly held shoe is a right or a left. Conjurers have been using methods of substitution since the first shamans discovered the trade-off.

Whatever your method, there is no excuse for any Satanic witch to compromise her glamour, if she has that potential. Far from being more vulnerable in spike heels, she is actually more intimidating to men who have perhaps never encountered a "real woman." Combine this with the insidious weaponry provided by an article of clothing unique in its exclusion from unisex fashion. Next time some creep gets out of hand, try threatening him with your tennis shoe or Birkenstock and see how far it gets you. Of course, you can always run. But too many women have been doing that for too long.

No Minors Allowed

It has been noted that children who exhibit a higher degree of intelligence favor music in minor keys. There is little question why. Minor keys, being more "sad" sounding, encourage introspection and serious thought. Bright major keys don't make the listener think, but only respond—largely to rhythmic, rather than lyrical content.

During my years spent playing the piano and organ before the public, it became easy to categorize and match people to music. Especially in bars, where restraints are reduced—it got so I could almost identify a requested selection before the customer even asked for it. In fact, so accurate was that faculty, that I could play a selection "to" a particular patron, and be sure of a response along the lines of "How did you know I was going to ask you for that number?"

Of all the categories of patrons matched to music, none was more consistent than what I came to term "The Menopausal Hit Parade," or "The Menopausal Top Ten." The musical selections in this category had a universal appeal to women over 40. The nature of the tunes had certain shared characteristics. They were all in major keys with either banal melodies or dissonant phrases which seemed to reinforce anxiety and frustration—melodies left hanging in places or with an air of incompletion. Examples include "Fascination" (flirtatious),

"Tenderly" and "All the Way" (heavy-handed romance), "These Boots are Made for Walking" (protest), "Downtown" and "The Stripper" (desperate emancipation), "Calcutta" and "Raindrops Keep Falling on My Head" (coquettish). All these songs exhibit a return to teenage values; a second childhood where things were never actually so extreme as in later years. And all are in major keys.

Rarely would I encounter an older woman who specifically requested a song in a minor mode. So firmly ingrained is an emphasis on youth, that an association, however unconscious, with the melancholy nature of minor music and death cannot be overlooked. Funeral marches, all being in minor keys, are seldom enjoyed by the elderly. Young people seem to have no problem with them, however.

A factor not to be overlooked is that most people who frequent cocktail lounges are trying to abate an inner pain. Many are alcoholics who are on the lam from life's commitments. Minor music leads to introspection and fosters brooding. Women who are afraid of aging and seek to escape its stigma don't want reminders of fading charms. They crave the exuberant love of adolescent romance more than ever. Seriousness is the mark of the crone. Minor music, by its very nature, is serious music. Here we have a paradox. Women in their twenties and thirties are prone to accentuate and enhance the seriousness of an affair. As they grow older, there is a swing towards light-hearted frivolity as "it makes me feel so young." Giddy old ladies don't care for minor music. Not at all.

The cliche "No sad songs for me" has a reason. So does the barroom plaint, "Let's liven things up here!" When youth dies, foolishness sets in. That's why there's no fool like an old fool.

Stereo: Scam of the Century

Q. What is the difference between army food and stereo?

A. One is canned Spam, and the other is panned scam.

The birth of stereo brought about the death of real musical appreciation. Before stereo, there was High Fidelity: an enhancement of recorded music. Hi-fi brought new realism to recorded music. Stereo brought new audio tricks but *less* musical realism. Stereo is such a given, so accepted and *expected,* that no one questions it, let alone criticizes it.

Unless one is sitting in the midst of an orchestra, there is invariably a *monophonic* source of any music heard, performed either collectively or individually. Live music may be performed stereophonically, but it's heard monophonically. Though music has been recorded in stereo for many years, most live music is heard from a single definable origin, by two ears mounted on a single head, attached to one body. Ears working in a pair act as range finders for sound, as do two eyes seeing a single object. Thus, most music, whether played by symphony orchestra, solo pianist, or bagpiper, is heard *binaurally,* whether the sound source is an ensemble or a single voice. "Stereophonic" refers to the source, rather than the receptor. "Monaural," as applied to musical listening, is a misnomer. It means "heard by only one ear," a condition exclusive to the aurally challenged.

If a sound source is stationary, it will be heard emanating from its point of origin. This applies to any ensemble, as well as single sound. Stereo supporters proclaim that each instrument of an orchestra can be defined and thus, better appreciated. They obviously listen to music for analysis rather than enjoyment. The dynamics of music require a balance of melody, harmony, and rhythm. When a homogenization of the three elements occurs, as with stereo reproduction (and even more democratically with digitally processed stereo), a great performance becomes a clockwork chatter. Every nuance is heard with equal clarity, yet there is no strength of character provided by key passages cutting through a harmonious wash. A flute becomes as stentorian as a trumpet; a triangle as distracting as a timpani roll. That is not listening to music. It's listening to individual sounds quarreling with each other to be heard. More than anything else though, it gives a consumer an opportunity to demonstrate his expensive equipment.

The scam of stereo was sold by proving its worth, which was a simple matter when presented to simple consumers. The sounds of passing trains, pipe organs (the only musical instrument actually capable of being played *and* heard stereophonically), birds, storms, race cars, swarms of crickets, troops passing in review, and ping pong matches, convinced anyone who had two functioning ears that just about *anything* sounded better emanating in stereo (or quadraphonic or octaphonic, for that matter). And it does. Just about anything, that is, but singing, speaking, or music.

I find it interesting that of all audible sounds, the overall quality of the aforementioned three has significantly declined since the advent of "stereo." Is it coincidence, or a cultural trade-off?

I recognize certain limited applications of stereo. If I want to listen to Alpine horns blowing on a glacier with my left ear, and the villagers singing down below with my right ear, then I can really appreciate stereo, thank you very much. Otherwise, give me one nice big speaker, one nice little speaker, and sufficient power to drown out unwanted conversation, and I'm perfectly satisfied. And one more thing I almost forgot: good music.

UR-Song
or Why There Are No
More Volume Pedals

Here are some of my secrets of music. They seem simple, and they are.

If you play a keyboard, use a volume pedal, also known as a swell pedal or expression pedal. Making music is a form of expression. An expression pedal is all but unknown today. To use one, you must know how to express your feelings. To express your feelings, it helps if you have some.

Touch sensitivity or velocity control is not a substitute for a volume control, and it never can be. "Touch sensitivity" sounds impressive; it bestows delusions to a callous lout that he has deep feelings. Velocity control is a trick to sell keyboards. All it controls is the beginning of a note. But where do you go from there? Would you drive a car without a gas pedal? If you consider yourself a musician, you should put more emotion into your music than into your driving. And yet, you drive with a pedal and play music without one. You say the car will not go if you don't have a pedal—it will just stay in one place. I assume that means that once you put your finger on a key, the music will automatically keep going until you take your finger off the key, pedal or no pedal. My six-month-old son can do that. He can play non-stop, and it sounds better than most contemporary musicians. He doesn't use a volume pedal either, but it's because his feet won't reach one. His legs are shorter than most musicians'. If you want to play with the same range of expression as a six-month-old baby, read no further. If music is to compel, it must have subtle variations in intensity.

Most musicians play music like they eat or fuck. Shovel it in. Chew 'til full. Shove it in. Screw 'til finished. Musical tempo is usually either too fast or too slow. No dynamics. There is a term which describes variation in tempo according to what the immediate mood of the music dictates. It is called *rubato.* It makes the difference between whether the composition played is routine, or seductive. A strict tempo (routine) maintains the hearer's attention to whatever he is already doing, whether it is dancing, marching, working, or shopping. Rubato (seductive) diverts the hearer's attention from what he is doing and makes him *listen,* rather than merely *hear.* Because rubato is unpredictable, it is mysterious. It is the fascination exerted by the subtleties of a harem dancer or a snake charmer's movements to his cobra. It is sinuous rather than linear. It is the serpentine curve, rather than the clockwork jog. If music is to compel, it must have predictable melody and harmony, but unpredictable tempo. This does not mean unpredictable rhythm, but variation in the *speed* of the rhythm.

Most professional keyboard musicians are like most professional writers. They play or write by the pound. More is better. The more notes that can be squeezed into a chord, the better. They can transform a compelling tune into atonal hash in their attempts to validate their professionalism. Rather than striving for an economy of notes, distilling and refining harmony to its most potent essence, they exemplify Stan Laurel's brilliant comment, "Lots of weather we're having, isn't it?" When playing harmony, strive for meaningful notes, rather than more notes.

THE HORNS OF A DILEMMA

"Confound and confuse 'til the stars be numbered." Perhaps this simple picture can be used as an example: a young boy coming home from school clutching a copy of *The Satanic Bible* in one hand and an LP of Al Jolson numbers in the other. How can a parent appropriately react to such a situation? An insurmountable problem becomes uncomfortably clear. The parent can't condemn the child for enthusiasm for Jolson's songs, but can condemn him for his interest in *The Satanic Bible.* Yet, what if the child sees the two as inseparably linked? To the media-saturated public it's irresolvable. But how does a parent calmly explain that to a militantly Satanic 13-year-old?

We are living in a new land of opportunity. As Satanists, we know one of the keys to success is an unflinching belief that there are no rules. Anyone who's ever succeeded has gone on that premise; not buying established procedures, business or otherwise. The naysayers are inevitably left behind amid shouts of "it cannot be done" and "should not be done"; claims that something won't receive distribution, won't receive acclaim, will never be accepted by the public.... There are so many good books to be written with Satanic themes, so many movies to be made—in the motion picture industry alone, the streets are again paved with gold. Experts will tell you, you can't have the Satanists win, they can't be the good guys. Why not? What rules are there that say that you can't? It's simply a given that it can't be done—it's one of those unwritten laws that says that all Satanists must advocate evil and must perform evil acts. Of course, that's what the new cottage industry to bolster the multi-billion dollar support system for Christianity has been provided with—the presumption that Satanists are evil for evil's sake and that through unmitigated evil acts the Devil's favorites receive all kinds of benefits. It ain't necessarily so. And because it ain't necessarily so, the dilemma should be exploited. It's a disservice not only to commerce, to the economy, but to individual initiative not to exploit these cracks in the established belief system.

If a person writes a screenplay wherein the protagonist, who happens to be a Satanist, has admirable and heroic qualities; and all of the most vile, slimy, malicious, insensitively stupid traits are possessed by the so-called "good" people, there's no rule against that. Yet anyone will say "You could never get such a film distributed." Possibly not. But I believe so. I believe that if it's different, if it's packaged and if it's there, someone will grab it and exploit it simply on the strength that it is untoward, that it hasn't been done before. It's just desperation on the part of those whose vested interests depend upon established standards that someone might take the ball and run with it—to a new playing field—that keeps such movies off the screens. We must realize that these prevailing dilemmas, these terrors that exist in the minds of the status quo are the only obstacles that keep new avenues from emerging on the scene.

The same elements of dilemma are presented and maintained in the musical world. It's assumed that generic popular music is rock—classic rock, quality rock, old-time rock, punk rock, acid rock, Rock of Ages rock—anything as long as it's "rock," to the point where it's become the generic. The only alternative to "Satanic rock" are outfits like Stryper who obviously are making no headway whatsoever. They're just different sizes of the same style shoe. Our Satanic objective is to confound, confuse, to create dilemma—to set up a revision-ist type of music that is basically a return to the old classical format, the disciplines, the romantic era of music; in which music has form, it has melody, it has harmony, it has rhythmic structure that can be grasped, that can indelibly impress itself upon the mind through the ears of the listener. If this kind of music is brought back under the banner of Satanism, and it's suitably packaged, no matter how outra-geously; someone, somewhere is going to exploit it, on the merits of its strengths, of its very form, of its cohesiveness, of its discipline, of its emotional impact and effect upon the listener. It cannot help but avalanche, overwhelming whatever form the generic rock has pre-sented so far. Rock has had its day. There's very little variation one way or the other. The only way music can change is in a 180° direc-tion to discipline, form, melody, harmony, lyricism, romanticism .... "Bombastic."

That's why bombastic music, which has dynamics and produces a gut reaction, is bound to overwhelm the current generic rock scene. Of course we're talking about billions of dollars in vested interests. There's going to be extreme pressure to curtail the new generic—"bombastic music"—as there has been in the recent past. A December 1, 1987, *Rolling Stone* article titled "Skinhead Nation" provides thinly-disguised fear-filled wailing in its dire warning. Along with reprehensible mis-quotes and misrepresentations, the writer makes snide references to the new skinhead music being "reductive, bombastic and self-con-scious" with "slower tempos and more conventional melody," "simple pub sing-along, catchy and monotonous." (What could be more monotonous than the linear cruise control of rock?) Bombastic is not going to be made easily available through the "experts" in musical retailing, merchandising, wholesaling. Obviously there's too much money being made already on the established formula. The new form of music is going to have to be produced as a labor of love, a packag-ing enterprise, irrespective of the money that can be made off of it. Once the engramatic idea, the emotional impact, of this kind of music has been indelibly etched in the mind of the listeners, it cannot help but be exploited. Those who support generic rock will drop it like a hot potato and scurry to this new musical form as soon as it's made acceptable.

Again, we will have presented the establishment with a dilemma. Of course we have to force the card—to back them against the wall and make damn sure in a filibustering sense that they know this is Satanic music. One way we can filibuster is by entering the established arena with something else that's outrageous enough or different enough to create a time slot, and then halfway through an interview or talk show, present this horrible additive of Satanism. A person going on a television show to plug a book on gaining weight for health might inject a few leading comments or be wearing a lapel pin with a Satanic symbol, the meaning of which might be questioned by the interviewer. Upon the revelation that the writer is also a Satanist, of course the remainder of the interview would be compulsively directed towards Satanism. They could no longer ignore the issue. The show would be sharply divided into two distinct subjects. That's how we can create dilemma.

The rest is easy. On one hand hysterics and experts will be screeching, "How can I protect my children from Satanism?" while, on another channel, the audience has already heard from Satanists that Satanism advocates listening to Rudy Vallee and Russ Columbo, Bizet, Rimsky-Korsakov, Sousa, Liszt; reading James Fenimore Cooper, Jack London, Mark Twain, Horatio Alger; and supporting Walt Disney.

Browning, Kipling, Romantic poets and writers of the heroic school; and certain contemporary writers like W. Somerset Maugham and Ben Hecht may not be considered Satanic until it is forced upon the listener or viewer that they *are* Satanic. Then, when there's the inevitable challenge, "Well, these writers aren't Satanic," it's *our* turn to take umbrage—we can be the offended party. We can be the ones to start bashing (symbolically, of course). If enough public Satanists are tough, vocal, and potentially dangerous (not mealy-mouthed, ivory-tower scholars), then it becomes a case of the 250-pound canary—when it sings, you listen.

That's where force and clout have to be waiting in the wings. As a reactionary or revisionist movement, when our long fuse burns out, that's the time to swing into action. Dilemmas reach an impasse only when your detractor is forced up against the wall and can't squirm away. As a result, once others say, "Well, that's not real Satanism, you're not real Satanists—you're just religious Satanists. The real Satanists are out killing babies and sacrificing cats"—that's our cue to start knocking heads. We have to be prepared to say "God damn it, you rotten sons of bitches! Don't tell me what Satanism is. I'm a *'real'* Satanist and I'm proud of it. You're trying to tell me Rudy Vallee isn't Satanic music, when I like Rudy Vallee?!" and then proceed to smash a chair over their head (or nose). Then they'll listen. That's the only way anyone who is still trying to make money off anti-Satanic swill will listen—when we stop defending ourselves and start being offensive.

That's why the ideal type of front-line warrior for our present cabal, for our new world view, must be that strange combination of berserker and poet. He must have the ultimate sense of justice, Lex Talionis, indelibly bred into him; while also possessing the articulation, the convictions, the ideals and the awareness of what must be done. These two elements of force and direction must be inseparable. Of warfare and intellect. One without the other is only productive on either a directionless or paper level. We've seen enough of what paper-pushers can do and effects they have by way of dialogue in written communication. The pen may still be mightier than the sword, but a broadsword can do much damage to a computer keyboard. What we have are people that can get out there and, to use the cliché, charismatically affect people in direct confrontations, in personal interchange, in public arenas. It's also why the new type of super-woman as well as the superman must be one of Charlie's girls raised to the ninth power, not just simply some strung-out, latter-day hippie or a dingaling that may have come from a promising background but got lost somewhere along the way on Haight Street. They have to be women that can out-woman the polyester droolers in studio audiences; out-woman the kind of women who would shrink and cringe at what they have to say; out-woman the non-women, or half women or partial women that can't quite make up their minds whether they're women or some kind of injection-molded plastic creations of a consumer society. In this way, the Satanists themselves become dilemmas, integrating factors that are supposed to be irreconcilable, and presenting alternatives that are supposed to be irresolvable. That's the strongest, and most dangerous power the Devil has. Now's the time to use that Satanic power to blast the last bastions of the weak-minded and soulless hordes.

How the Devil Raises Hell

The ground rule is to take a person's indulgences (they have very few, life-hating as they are) and give them more than they bargained for.

"Is it hot enough for you?" people ask, meta-talking to a friend on an unbearably hot day. Most people can never be warm enough, for they are as cold and dead as they will always be. They need heat. Not in moderation. They can never do anything in moderation. That's why I roast, while they are just comfortable. So I give them heat. I put them in a room to wait for me, and turn up the heat to over 100 degrees. When they are quite warm, I make my appearance. By that time, they are so debilitated that they can't think straight and will agree to anything.

Do they want love, sex, or similar gratification? I give them high hopes. I promise them delights, knowing that once they get what they want, they will no longer want it. Unused as they are to receiving genuine love or concern, they wouldn't recognize the real thing if they had it, much less know what to do with it. If I wish to curse them, I send them love in the form of an overly ardent suitor. Nothing is as pesky or exasperating as unwanted attention. When they send out a call for love, and I want to torture them, I provide someone whom they soon wish would go away.

My sleep habits are subject to change without notice. When they say "The Devil never sleeps," what they don't know is that he does indeed sleep, and best, when they are most active. I receive others during their sleep hours. Much like the aforementioned heat treatment, I choose to receive visitors at the exact time that normally energetic people must relinquish their exuberance. I make sure that they are too tired to properly function by giving them lots of anticipation time. Unable to relax during my sleep time, they burn themselves out before they confront me. In that manner, I give them more meaningful time with me. By "meaningful," I mean that every minute seems to them an hour, so tired are they. It also means that in indulging them my time, I am being mean.

Anything I can excel at, is an abrasive reminder of others' incompetence. Rather than engender instant animosity, I flatter up their non-existent abilities. In this way I pump up their egos, continuously threatened as they are by the competitive needs of their peers. If they can sing one song, and badly, I tell them they are great singers. They want to excel, so I provide approbation. Then they go their way, cawing and screeching, and are soon shouted down by their fellows. Thus, they are made more miserable than ever, and I have punished them for their pretentiousness.

If they want power, I encourage their dreams of leadership. I know that they will grab the bait. Their anti-charisma precludes them from amassing any followers. Their only hope is to steal followers from me, and their true thieving nature comes out. At best, they siphon off the kind of disciples I don't want. Then they are stuck with them, and I am rid of them, and soon they are at each others' throats. By providing them sovereignty, albeit dubious, I give them more than they bargain for.

These are but a few of my devices. I have many others. They all have one thing in common: I give them Hell though it appears to be gratification. After all, why shouldn't I? I have seen how ungrateful they can be. The guy upstairs is always understood and thanked, even for calamity. The Devil is always blamed, even though he may be truly charitable.

THE JEWISH QUESTION?
OR THINGS MY MOTHER
NEVER TAUGHT ME

Now that Satanism has rained on so many parades by advancing a "Third Side" to most convenient and established dichotomies, it's time to question the "Jewish Question." There are conflicting factors which would infuriate sob-sister liberal Identity Jews, as well as myopic Identity Christian Jew-haters. Here are some inconvenient things to think about:

According to H.L. Mencken, prior to 1936 there were 65 people in the New York phone book named "Hitler," "Hiedler," or "Hütler," 61 of whom were Jewish. As might be expected, within a short time, all had vanished. It seems "Hitler" was not the most ingratiating name to have in the U.S. at that time. Studebaker automobiles had a fine big "Dictator" model, which they were forced to rename, because Americans suddenly developed an aversion to the word "Dictator." Many historians have advanced Adolf's own suspected Jewish background as grounds for his "overcompensation"; as was often observed, he certainly would have been unable to pass Aryan racial standards of hair and eye coloring and nose length. Did Charlie Chaplin have a Hitler moustache, or vice versa?

Reinhard Heydrich, however, would have passed as the blonde, blue-eyed epitome of Nordic aesthetic standards. The only problem was that Heydrich's detractors' constant weapon against him (including blackmail) was his "Jewish origins."

As Ken Anger and others have pointed out, "Little Joe" Goebbels and Eddie Cantor appear to have been "separated at birth." Totally non-Aryan-type Goebbels also had a clubfoot, which could have stigmatized him as "a deformed Jewish cripple" by Nazi genetic standards.

Erhard Milch, former director of Lufthansa, who became, with Hermann Goering, head of the Luftwaffe until the fall of the Third Reich, was one of the "Aryanized." So was Fritz Todt, inventor of the *autobahn* (now called the freeway) and Minister of Armaments and Munition. Karl Haushofer's suspected Jewish origins didn't lessen the liability of his Jewish wife, and their son, Albrecht, advisor to Rudolf Hess.

I won't even touch upon the saga of Eric Jan Hanussen, long-time pal of Hitler's, originator of *Die Elektrischenvorspiele,* acknowledged Black Magus of the Third Reich, and referred to as "The Rasputin of Germany."

The most embarrassing scandal, as chronicled in Viereck's *Metapolitics: The Roots of the Nazi Mind,* occurred in 1938 when it was proven beyond reasonable doubt that Richard Wagner's real father was not his mother's husband, Frederick Wagner, but a Jewish matinee actor, Ludwig Geyer, who lived with Frau Wagner and whom she married after Herr Wagner's death. Nietzsche, among others, had seen the composer's unretouched draft of Richard's autobiography naming Geyer as his father. The story broke in the *New York Times* (the same as with Dan Burros many years later) on July 8, 1939, and some fancy footwork was in order for the Nazis to get the stage redressed. By that time the world recognized Wagner as the composer laureate of the Reich.

The point to be made here is not one of right or wrong, good or evil, but of Third Side Satanic awareness. In 1934, after negotiating with Zionist leaders, Josef Goebbels had a special commemorative medal struck, bearing the Swastika on one side and the Star of David on the other. Many such "inconsistencies" are cited in Lenni Brenner's *Zionism in the Age of the Dictators.* This is not intended as any sort of revisionism, but Satanic food for thought. The strange alliances which accompanied the development (and growth) of Israel could fill several volumes alone, not including many other seeming inconsistencies in Nazi machinations.

What's a little holocaust among friends? The Holocaust needs no revisionism, when one considers the Satanic Third Side, *Oberkommandos* notwithstanding. Japan "lost" the war, but seems to be making out just fine, thank you, though Port Chicago and Nagasaki were holocausts of a different variety. (Did you know that the inventors, designers and builders of the atomic bomb were almost all Jews? They were from many countries; Germany, Italy, Denmark—and they were "allowed" to "escape" to the U.S. to do the job, rather than work in Germany. Even the Air Force bombardier who sighted in and actually released The Bomb was Jewish.)

The first time I read the Protocols of the Elders of Zion, my instinctive reaction was, "So what's wrong with THAT? Isn't that the way any master plan should work? Doesn't the public deserve—nay, demand—such despotism?" What we see around us now proves it beyond a doubt, just as Orwell, McLuhan, and Mander projected, and Spencer long before them. Both Perry London in *Behavior Control* and Roger Price in *The Great Roob Revolution* drew up the blueprints. What is "tyranny"? Despotism? Is it all so bad, if so attractively packaged that it's demanded? Does the mental capacity and general well-being of the public not thrive under it? I see no great mass of free-thinkers around ME. Where are they hiding? Certainly not on a drill field of trendiness.

Getting back to the Jews: was not Torquemada, the father of the Inquisition and original Jew buster, himself of Jewish origin? Think about it.

So was Benjamin Disraeli, Britain's empire builder who, as Queen Victoria's Prime Minister, raised British imperialism to its most romantic and legendary heights.

So was Bernardino Nogara, the Italian-Jewish gold trader who was hired to save the Vatican from financial ruin at the turn of this century.

The list seems endless.

There used to be a poem that went: "Roses are reddish/Violets are bluish/If it wasn't for Jesus/We'd all be Jewish." Well, maybe not quite, but there's a lot that has historically been dealt under the table and you don't have to be a 33° Mason to speculate. Whether you choose to follow the example of Tamerlane or Albert Schweitzer, the choice as a Satanist is yours. Odinism is an heroic and admirable form of Satanism, as is an affinity for Coyote or Vlad Tepes. Just remember: Things are not always what they appear to be.

In 1834 the German-Jewish philosopher Heinrich Heine prophesied an atavistic return to the "primitive powers of Nature that would evoke the demoniac energies of Germanic pantheism.... Should the subduing talisman, the Cross, break, then will come roaring forth the wild madness of the old champions, the insane Berserker rage, of which the northern poets sing. That talisman is brittle, and the day will come when it will pitifully break. The old stone gods will rise from the long-forgotten ruin and rub the dust of a thousand years from their eyes; and Thor, leaping to life with his giant hammer, will crush the Gothic cathedrals!"

Panty Pissers:
A New Perspective On
An Old Fetish

More than ever before, fetishism is a dominant factor in sex in the Western world. It used to be that fetishism was considered a compulsive, less-than-perfect substitute for "normal" sexual activity. At its best, fetishism was a motivating adjunct to traditional copulation. The "danger" of advanced fetishism was that it could serve as a preferable substitute for healthy sex, the fetish serving as the end-all and be-all. Like masturbation, it was claimed to discourage, if not eliminate, any chance of a "healthy, normal relationship."

Now, there are fewer disease-free outlets for sexual gratification. Before, if one masturbated, it was to hide one's sexual demands in a world wherein actual sexual activity outside of marriage was proscribed. Now, one of the advantages of masturbation is relative safety from the ravages of rampant sexual disease. Advocacy of masturbation is in direct contrast to the horrors attributed to it early in the 20th century. In other words, the same fetishes are there but they are now openly encouraged (and profited by).

The particular fetish addressed here is now called *elective inconti-*

nence. It is sexual excitement derived from wetting oneself, and is practiced almost exclusively by women. It was an integral part of sexual expression during a repressive age, but was always "in the closet."

Today, there is less emphasis placed upon copulation and more importance given to gratification, by whatever form taken. Fantasy plays a bigger part than ever. It is less important to satisfy a partner than to satisfy oneself. Hence, the "solitary vice" has arrived. Foreplay is unnecessary to a sexual encounter if there is no actual encounter, let alone culmination in a mutual sexual act.

Foreplay takes on a new meaning when the ultimate result is solitary gratification. Foreplay becomes anticipation, planning, timing, and setting, preparatory to the act of urinating in one's panties. A well-planned, well-executed public spectacle is a goal of the most dedicated panty pissers.

Panty pissing is a fetish which gives pleasure to the viewer but, more importantly, to the perpetrator. It need not serve as a prelude to sexual intercourse but rather as an exciting and gratifying act in and of itself. This is in large part due to the symbology and motivations behind the act.

Elective incontinence is no more dependent upon follow-through sexual intercourse than is fellatio dependent upon vaginal contact. Surely, no criticism dare be leveled at homosexual activity on the grounds that it does not require a man and a woman for its performance.

Panty pissing is largely masturbatory. It provides a male viewer with visions upon which to speculate and take into hand, both during and long after the incident. The flavor lasts. Once seen, never forgotten.

It bestows an unrivaled set of erotic stimuli upon the performer, with a range encompassing fear and apprehension; anxiety and desperation; withholding, denial, and eventual release; shame and humiliation; overwhelming embarrassment; abandon and degradation; flagrant naughtiness and rebellion; and spite and assertion.

Above all, an entire scenario can be stagecrafted and controlled by the performer yet, as in days of yore, without anyone the wiser. The thrill is more than temporal, for it is the stuff of which lasting fantasies are made. One well-executed act of incontinence is good for countless strong masturbatory reminiscences. In fact, the performance itself is often highly embarrassing and unsavory, but future reflection becomes material for the most heightened sexual fantasies imaginable. There seems to be a rule that the most traumatizing performances, once completed and upon reflection, yield the most intense orgasms.

Magical power is conferred to the performer, in that she will be remembered as well as had she played the lead in a legitimate theatrical performance. The amount of energy thrown her way by witnesses to her embarrassment, in residual thought forms, is phenomenal. That is because the viewers, too, share her embarrassment, and are thus drawn into the actuality of the tableaux. The persistence of memory in those she has affected can only be hinted at. The taboo she has violated, though harmless enough, rivals scenes of carnage and wholesale destruction as would be retained in the mind's eye.

Why Walk?

"That's the way it's always been!"

Man cannot evolve with that attitude.

The other day I was walking around in a museum, thinking about how close my physical activity was to that of spending the same amount of time at Disneyland. Why, I wondered, was I expending all this energy to see things others might see on a TV special or computer program, all the while sitting comfortably like couch potatoes.

You're thinking: "But that's not like actually being there and seeing the real thing." In other words, I must stand and walk to see "real thing," whereas virtual reality allows me to sit during the entire experience.

Man became Homo Erectus because he could evolve no further under then-existing conditions. Just because he still ambulates on his hind legs doesn't bestow some superior intelligence. His mind, having evolved (?) has invented the wheel. It has also invented solar, nuclear, electric, magnetic, steam, internal combustion, and other forms of power. He is enabled to ride in mini-vans shaped like Buckminster Fuller envisioned, rather than behind or on top of another animal who pulls him, utilizing all four legs, rickshaws excepted.

In a burst of human interaction, I commented to a man in a wheelchair, how he had it made because he could sit comfortably while everybody else in the place had to lurch around on their hind legs. To me, he replied: "Oh, I can walk just fine, but why bother?"

I pondered that comment the rest of the day. The guy was breaking no laws, bothering no other people, but was terribly dishonest with society. Yet he was completely truthful with me. Why should he ride while others had to walk. The answer finally came to me. It was this: Because he COULD. He had discovered his own way of beating the system—of getting special advantages without expending any effort or money. In reality, he was just a few years ahead of his time.

Women don't show their legs in public any more, despite their exercise attempts to improve that area of their anatomy. Most sex is either procreative (horizontal) or elective (sedentary). The urge is no respecter of physical fitness dependent upon getting about on two legs.

Airports have had people-movers for a long time. The conveyer belts enable passengers to stand still and relax, some even having folding seats along the sides. Facilities for the handicapped have become expected. Wheelchairs were just the beginning. I foresee a time—soon—when only chumps will walk. They will appear as awkward in public as a dog or cat getting about on its hind legs. Or someone on the freeway driving a horse and buggy.

The logistics are simple. Emission-free personal conveyances will take up no more space than pedestrian traffic. Public arenas (theaters, etc.) need have no seats; each patron enters and leaves with their own. Ramps will be universal, replacing stairways. Business will flourish, as there will be no fatigue from shopping, nor problems carrying purchases.

Inclement weather presents no problem, as clear plastic bubbles similar to existing bicycle and motorcycle helmets can cover the operator. Portability and storage when not in use is limited only to the inventiveness of space-saving construction. Folding and telescoping, rechargeable powered, small-wheeled conveyances can be made to reduce in size and bulk to no larger than a briefcase.

Identification methods are already capable of monitoring the individual, so it is reasonable to assume that conveyance operators and their whereabouts can be monitored, much as computers can monitor their users via the internet. Automobiles already have tracking devices in the guise of locating a motorist in distress.

Personal computers can be taken everywhere, thus surfing the nets can be as easy as pulling one's pod off to the side of the sidewalk. Not having to actually carry their computers, operators will be encouraged to snap them onto their conveyances. They need never be more than a power switch away from worldly interaction.

Actual walking—or pedestrian locomotion—need only occur within the confines of one's own dwelling. Retention of muscle tone is obtainable through many personalized means and devices. If man was not intended to sit most of the time, he would not be made with such a big fat ass. So, more power to it!

Don't Be A Slave To (⊙ther's) Subliminals

We live in a world of subliminals. If no one has an original thought, it's understandable. External influences permeate our lives. For most, it's TV or other media. No one will ever know the extent to which subliminal suggestion controls our lives. Silence seems to be the only retreat; sensory deprivation the only conscious alternative.

Yet, the sound of silence itself is often the most disturbing of all. It's not so much that silence releases an "inner voice" which is often too disturbing to hear. Even if one is fortunate enough to be able to live with his unreleased thoughts, there are always other distractions, far more depleting than personal misgivings. For example: in the absence of external stimuli, including subliminals, one becomes more acutely aware of the workings of his own body. Every ache and pain, however slight, is magnified into an event. A slight tickle, unnoticed if watching TV, will become an insurmountable itch without the distraction. A gurgling moment of indigestion, not even felt while preoccupied with external stimuli, becomes a threatening cancer.

Part of this phenomena is caused by our living in a world of preoccupying distraction. There are so many sounds that permeate our lives in a machine-gun manner, the brain can no longer cope with slow—or no—thoughts upon which to concentrate. Just as nature abhors a vacuum, the mind must fill space, even if it's to practice meditation or to enter an alpha state.

Volitional thought is only as independent as external messages will allow it to be. A possible solution? Create your own subliminals. Custom craft your own distractions. Whether audio or visual, provide your mind with things to think about and, more importantly, to respond to. Make an audio cassette tape of subliminal messages that can benefit only you. Employ sound producers designed to permeate your space with backgrounds upon which your mind can focus. A sound of crickets is better in the background than a chattering TV, and serves the same purpose: it gives your mind something upon which to focus.

It is both inaccurate and foolish to listen to inane or meaningless radio or TV because it will put you to sleep. The producers of those entertainments are unconcerned that you sleep through their commercials. In fact, if you do; all the better. You're more receptive to whatever messages are sent. The pacing is designed to wear you out. Unlike vaudeville, where an act that put the audience to sleep would find few bookings, a TV or radio show can be more successfully designed as soporific rather than conscious entertainment.

Is it any wonder that so many people "sleep through their jobs"? Still, they complain "I can't be how I'd like to be—I have to WORK for a living." What they really mean is: "I have to be preoccupied in order to live." Work gives them focus, dignity, and acceptability. No matter how objectionable, their work fills a void that would be like silence to others. And it exposes them to the instructional messages their co-workers receive. The only thing worse than idle hands is an idle mind. Your Masters have eliminated that possibility. Wouldn't it be better if YOU could?

THE REAL VICTIMS

The cult of the victim has been identified. The pedagogy of the oppressed. Everyone at a loss because of past abuse. Someone to blame. Always someone to blame. A neglect, an abuse, a molestation. An alcoholic father. Mother. Parents. Born black. Born gay. Made gay. Misunderstood. Slow learner. Battered. Abducted. Satanic survivor. Unwanted child. Everybody's a victim. There's always someone else to blame. Sue the doctor. Sue the teacher. Sue the boss. Sue the company. Sue the parents.

These are not the real victims. These are not the real casualties of war. The children, the innocent, the harmonious, the naive. They are the real victims. I know. I was married to one for a quarter of a century. When she needed medication for a real mid-life change, she got rhetoric instead. Massive doses of cant from experts in victimization. She was weak. Not very bright in the uses and forms of treachery. She was tough in spirit, but weak in guile. She didn't have to be guileful. There were plenty of others who did her chicanery for her. Lawyers, counselors. All with horror stories of their own. All knowing and recovering victims. Gauleiters in the army of the destruction of the innocents.

The women's movement destroyed naiveté, and in so doing, it annihilated innocence. The malcontents versus the satisfied. The ugly versus the beautiful. And the malcontent and the ugly were to become the official victims from which the scam of oppression would emerge and flourish.

"You're not really happy—you just think you are because your eyes haven't been opened to the way you've been used." "You're not really happy" became a command, not an analysis.

More long-term relationships were dissolved during the '80s than during any other period in civilized history.

Greed and its resultant consumerism provoked the war. If two could live as cheaply as one, a waning economy necessitated a drastic change. The battle cry was: "Break up the marriages." The rest is now history.

There will always be professional victims. The entire concept of Christianity is a victim cult. To be Christ-like is to be victimized and concurrently righteous. The women's movement is but another last-ditch device to perpetuate the nobility of oppression. It is a campaign in their Armageddon. Like all warfare, it has its casualties. And like warfare, it is ruthless and the bombs fall on all.

The women's movement and the cult of the victim are Christian ploys.

They are inexorably linked.

The real casualties of this war are the satisfied, the stoical, the responsible, the placid, the female archetype. Manufactured insecurities are the weaponry of this war. Rifles are replaced by false counsel, delivered by tongues as poisonous as curare-tipped spears. Breaking rifles is not enough, nor is trying to defuse bombs. Tongues must be silenced even if it means lopping off heads. A reversal is in order. A fresh dichotomy to the women's movement/cult of the victim/Christian holdouts is imperative. It must be more ruthless in its methodology, more dramatic than the now-mainstream absorptions of the enemy. It must truly liberate, with real women at the helm—not dissatisfied pawns of a failing economy. The old casualties are permanent. The wires have been cut and the dirt has been thrown over their graves and no amount of mourning will bring them back. But the stragglers of the army of their destruction can and must be destroyed without mercy. As the last Christians they represent, they must be jeered and ridiculed, for their non-existent humor cannot begin to defend them. They have done the dirty work for their undetected Masters, and now, like obsolete soldiers, they must be cashiered. Their victims may have been weak, but they are stupid and their past stupidity must take its toll on their residual smugness.

If the new warrior-woman can enjoy degradation as an elective, its demonstrated existence will wither the enemy. In its self-righteousness and brittle rigidity, it will crumble as chalk figurines—pretentious, pompous masters they fancy themselves. Their whips are limp noodles. Their leather is melting licorice. Their spikes are french fries and their boots are oilcloth. And their men? Like all serfs, they will go the way of the new conquerors and take up the noodle whips and licorice gauntlets and maybe even learn to actually help a woman, other than bend to a whipping.

Recorded history will laugh at the temperance/Carrie Nation tactics of the Woman's Army of Emancipation of the twentieth century, but their damage has been done to the real victims of their folly. The cult of the victim will be seen for what it was, but the real casualties will never be recorded. This time their sisters will march with clear heads and a lesson well-learned. There must be constant reminders though. And enough security to overbalance the insecurities that felled past casualties. And anyone caught sowing seeds of sedition must be smashed into fertilizer.

The Genesis Of The Fuckup

Ineptitude Rules

As individual identities wane, there is an increasing use and contrived employment of ineptitude. When a person feels a loss of self esteem—despite encouragement provided by consumerism that he is special—what can he do to bolster his needs for recognition? After all, the whole objective of consumerism is to sell ego-boosting products so that the consumer feels All Right and is not ostracized from the herd. In order to achieve that purpose, the consumer must first be placed into a position of constant insecurity. His should be a fear of obsolescence. By enjoying the regeneration provided by his purchase of "new and improved" consumer goods, he will himself feel alive and vital.

Modern man does not live in a meritocracy. He is encouraged, instructed, and carefully nurtured to avoid trying to do things too well. He knows that excellence is a ticket to failure. Incompetence pays off. All around him, like the sound of the world, is evidence of mediocrity and ineptitude being rewarded. If one is too competent at something, he is ignored, if not despised and belittled. The formula for success is not to do something capably, but to do it noisily. Glaring ineptitude always wins out over quiet efficiency.

How Not To Want To Do Better

Is it any wonder that ineptitude has become an almost universal character trait? To one who receives insufficient recognition, it's easier and more productive to get attention by fucking up. Our society thrives on abrasiveness. Abrasion is the painful, masochistic need which has been proven to sell products. The most abrasive commercials are the ones best remembered and most heeded. Think about it. Far more time is spent complaining about disruptive things and abrasive people in one's life than in taking inventory of the positive. The squeaky wheel has never in man's history had so much oiling.

There was a time when very young children discovered they could get attention by doing the wrong thing, as much or more than by doing the right thing. If there was punishment, it was well worth the recognition gained. Fortunately, most kids, as they left infancy, learned that a reward system worked better. There was plenty of evidence, on many levels, that a meritocracy of sorts existed.

Lazy Warriors

Somewhere in the 1930s, calculated dissidence, by way of trade unions, began to chip away at that meritocracy. Among the lower classes a growing suspicion developed that diligence did not pay off. Consequently, physically hazardous labor strikes mellowed into the sit-down strike, which in turn spawned the fine art of gold bricking. For the young and/or uninitiated: a sit-down strike was a tactic by which angry workers demonstrated a form of passive resistance by sitting on the floor and not moving until their wage demands were met. It worked, because no violence ensued, yet traffic was impeded by the sitters. "Gold bricking" became a means to stay on a job while getting paid for sleeping. The second world war was a perfect proving ground, in that millions of GI's perfected the skill. Thereafter, the best job with the most secure employment was the soft job. If a job wasn't soft enough, it was no cause for concern. A little effort, using proper strategy, could make even a soft job a little softer.

The God of Assholes

God must have loved the common man, because He made so many of them. True, but let us not forget that man really creates his gods in accordance with his needs. Then, he finds solace (and importance) by pretending that his god created him. If God is a fuckup and an asshole, it's because of the most visible traits of his creators. Surely, if God is capricious, irresponsible, and mercurial, His children should behave no differently. That is why fucking up to get attention is a natural tendency, especially among those of little other consequence. The directive: "Don't just stand there; DO SOMETHING!" may be sound advice for survival in the work place. Increasing amounts of people have discovered greater identity in observing a new and improved formula for recognition. It goes: "Don't just do something; do it WRONG!" Just as the sit-down strike of yore paid off, the modern fuckup has found a voice.

Fake Discrimination

Grievance committees for hearing claims of racial and sexual discrimination and abuse—and unfair practices of all variety—ensure a forum for both the legitimate and the fake. Unfortunately, the forum is abused more than used. It becomes a hand-in-glove opportunity for fuckups of all variety. The procedure is effortless: a "worker" displays apparent incompetence, is chastised or otherwise treated accordingly, then runs to the nearest agency to file a complaint of "discrimination." Usually the outcome is a monetary settlement, and/or a return to the abusive job with preferred treatment. What started out as a slick but limited means of uncredited bunco, soon spread to upstanding and otherwise honorable workers. Popular media and its contagion soon produced a norm, and the little man (or woman) began learning tangible advantages of incompetence.

Negative Reinforcement

The outcome of incompetence, properly applied, is another's annoyance and discomfort. Like the child who received attention doing the wrong thing, adults have perfected the game. In addition to being rewarded for fucking up, they are noticed and, most of all, remembered. They receive enough magical energy from those they have annoyed to provide an identity and with it, tremendous gratification. Many don't fuck up all the time—just enough to maintain an omnipresent problem and a lasting impression. These are not the totally maladroit, but part-time fuckups who judiciously practice the art when needed. They make themselves indispensable, so when they fuck up, their ineptitude is glaring enough to be memorable. Thus, they have served their identity requirements. If it once was accepted that a little helplessness and ineptitude was an endearing trait—especially in women—it has reached heights of incompetence never dreamed of. Those who excel, fail—and are frustrated. Those who fail, excel—and are gratified. What would Professor Darwin think?

Writter's Disgust
by Anton "Tony" LaVey

$\dot{I}$t used to be said, "If you're so smart, why ain't you rich?" and professionalism was measured by an exchange of money for one's product. No one could be a professional unless he got paid for what he was doing. One short poem, *paid for* and published, constituted professionalism more than ten thousand pages of unsolicited, self-published writing. When amateur writers discovered the prestige of having their name in print, however, vanity publishers saw to it that anyone with enough money to spend could present himself as an author. Unfortunately, if one's writing stank, vanity publishing did little to establish professional status. Now, word processors and desktop publishing serve the same ends.

There are no more amateurs. Everyone is a pro, an expert. Just as computers and word processors have made anyone a writer, guitars and amplification gear have made anyone a musician. The very word "amateur" has become a pejorative, notwithstanding that it means someone who loves what they are doing. I suppose a message exists here. The motivation for being either a writer or a musician is prestige and acclaim, not love for the medium. That may explain the present level of competence in the world of literature and music.

Graphic art is a bit different. If a picture was once worth a thousand words, it must now be worth a million. Visually oriented as we humans are, representational art can still be evaluated by untrained eyes. Trees, horses and sailboats still look pretty much the same to one who knows what they're supposed to look like. There's not much room for fudging. Depictions of people might vary, but a nose is still expected to be in the middle of a face, which in turn, is anticipated to be above, not beneath the torso. Skillful drawing and painting is not dependent upon advanced technology or its consumer products. But wait a moment. Computer generated graphics have made it possible for even the most artistically bereft person to paint by number, elevated to its highest power. Photography no longer depends upon the instantaneous *capturing* of a situation on film, but on a *selection* made from myriad sequential images. Thus, a skilled and rapid coordination between the photographer's eye and the camera shutter becomes a thing of the past.

I have found that the most important ingredients in writing are content and controversy. Almost as important is a ready audience— but that can be dispensed with, for if content and controversy are strong enough, readership is assured. Millions of words have been written on the secrets of successful writing, most of them concentrating upon how to make for interesting reading. The most interesting reading is about tabooed people, things, or events. Of the three elements, sex, sentiment, and wonder; the wonder theme—that which most overtly frightens—is the most compelling. For better or worse, humans respond to fear and pain when all else fails. Timid little creatures that they are, they will rush *towards* the danger which threatens them, if they can remain safe at the same time. And *that* is the kind of stuff to write about. Prurience, vicariousness, scandal appeal to all. Content must be intriguing; i.e. scary. The most romantic love story is filled with fear. The more trial and tribulation, the more obstacles; the better. The gallery will always be filled with masochists. Such is the nature of the human animal.

Now that we have taken care of the real formula involved in being a proffessional writter, there are some things that must be added. This is asumming that you want to be a writter how ever. If you want to be an artist, as has been mentioned, their are computer generated graphics, which will make it not only possible but probibble. The old method of painting by numbers has come a long ways. Unfortunatly my spell checker and on board dictionary seems to have crashed but as can be seen, it does nothing to hamper my writting. If you have something to say than say it. A talented writter will find many market's open to him or herself. The most important thing to remember is, "Get it published." Once your work has been excepted, their will always be new demand's. Just as a musicians composition's will be heard (and they will, thanks to the mackerel of modern technology, sequencers, mixers, ect.) an excepted writters writting is *bound* to be read (smile).

Some Professionals and a Poem

The difference between a "highly skilled professional" and an ordinary "professional" is that the former gets paid for doing something while the latter just gets paid.

What does a young man do who wants to be a cop but can't stand the sound of a gun or the sight of blood? Who wants to be a musician but can neither carry a tune in a bucket, nor feel anything when he hears a good one?

He becomes a lawyer. Lawyers send a client out with more problems than when he came in. Their great talent is in obfuscation and casing the mark. They can be recognized by the sound of the equivocator; "Now, now!" They might even make fine Satanists—but on the other hand....

Doctors have learned that you can't make any money off a patient who's feeling well so you keep 'em sick. Send the patient out with more worries than when he came in. Now if you'll just take off your clothes....

Auto mechanics lack the schooling to be lawyers or doctors, yet depend on the desperation of those who depend on their cars. An automobile mechanic will always find something wrong with a car brought in for a checkup, and a very expensive solution for one that is not running.

Psychiatrists are doctors who don't like to keep washing their hands. When not being paid to listen, they charge money to tell you that you are not normal, and charge more money to tell you that you are. After lawyers get through with a client, he needs psychiatric help or else he will go to jail. Psychiatrists are probation officers with pipes and elbow patches. A man becomes a psychiatrist so he can call someone else crazy before they call him crazy.

Most "experts" aren't. Like "professionals," they can charge money for their services. Whatever you say to an expert will be right or wrong depending on who's paying him and how much. It matters little how much an expert actually knows. What really matters is his reputation as an expert, at which he works diligently. The only thing an expert is an expert at, is in providing himself with a reputation as an expert. That is my expert opinion.

Sociologists are people who get paid for looking at prostitutes and collecting dirty jokes.

All beauty consultants and fashion designers are ugly. Women who do their own hair are prettier than those who have it done by professionals. Professional hairdressers are either men who hate women, or reasonably attractive women who started out doing their own hair but can't stand a customer who looks better than themselves.

Most poets are wannabe writers who can't properly compose a sentence, much less write a story. Besides, it takes less time to write a few lines and put a frame around it. I'm a poet. I have written the world's shortest poem, called "Woman": Strife is/Life. (Three syllables.) Before I came along the world's shortest poem was "Fleas": Adam/Had 'em. (Four.) Most musical composers can't play music that's already been written and is well-known. If you play only your own compositions, no one can hear the mistakes. Nowadays there are a lot of poets and composers.

The first requirement of an occultist, seer, or psychic is a lack of any sense of humor. In a profession not likely to be taken seriously, it is disastrous to display levity. If you can't be serious, you can't expect to be taken seriously. For an occultist, seriousness is the easiest part. It comes naturally. It takes wit and intelligence to have a sense of humor. Occultniks have neither. They can't figure anything out. That is why they depend on their psychic abilities.

The scientist and the mystic can never get along. One tells stale jokes and the other doesn't get them.

Habit Dies Hard

The worst habit is easiest kept. When dealing with people, always recognize their wont, or habitual way of doing things. No matter how much one complains about his lot, habit will always win out. The way things are is the way you must allow them to continue. With modification, perhaps, but always adhering to the comfort of habit.

The only way to modify another's behavior is to do it within the framework of that to which they are comfortably accustomed. With most people, what you see is what you get—and will continue to get—with very little deviation. When someone talks of "turning over a new leaf," what they really mean is to replace the old one with another of the same kind.

Observe how habit triumphs when one mate is replaced by another. There's a reason why each successive partner bears significant similarities to those who have gone before. Habit. Comfortable, unbreakable habit.

The threat of success is ominous to most, because of the fear of new challenges which accompany it—even though success is indulgent and/or liberating. It is for this reason that it is unwise to try to "help" another who has led a life of failure and disappointment. When one is used to failure, there is a specious kind of comfort in more of the same.

Given their way, most people would never want change. The purpose in advertising and merchandising is to convince people that they cannot survive without new things in their lives. As a result, most lives are a series of frustrations engendered by unwanted change. After enough of this sort of conditioning, uncertainty and anxiety over obsolescence become themselves habitual. If you wish to make another happy, first ascertain whether or not their habit is based on flux, or stasis. This principle can be illustrated by the two alternatives of "replacement" or "upgrading." Bearing in mind that habit must be maintained at all costs, decide which means will best serve your subject.

If fear of obsolescence enslaves, you must provide your victim with "new and improved" (but only cosmetic) substitutes for that which is already ensconced—but always maintain what has become habit. Merchandisers know that resistance to break habit can be eliminated by "upgrading." That way, a habitually-used thing can be painlessly maintained, while assuaging pressure to "keep on top of things."

Though empires can be destroyed, the most difficult of all human creations to break is habit. Only through trickery can it be accomplished. I have employed a variation on the principle, "The best way to avoid temptation is to yield to it." I applaud another's bad habit and appear to be stimulated by it. Most people wish to have power over someone else. If, for example, I make it clear that I am stimulated by a woman who bites her nails, perversity equates to power. The subject will continue to bite her nails for a while. But then it will occur to her that if she stops, I will be upset. Rather than continue a habit which, though detrimental, is comforting, the subject will transfer her habit to me, like a sin eater. Though comforting to her, the habit seems to be even more important to me. Then, when I seem distressed that she doesn't bite her nails anymore, she discovers the power of denial. Her bad habit has become a weapon, whereby a greater indulgence exists in her newfound power. Unlike the breaking of habit for successful change, there is no additional responsibility incurred.

Though my subject may have considered herself inferior (the very insecurity caused the nail-biting in the first place), I have changed all that. I have provided a means whereby she has power over me by refusing to bite her nails! Her prior sadomasochistic rejection insurance, provided by chipped and jagged nails, has been transformed into a magical weapon—a power tool for denial. Thus, I have employed the unexpected, the unpredictable. Through the element of surprise, I have used the human foible of perversity to break a habit. No habit is strong enough to withstand approbation. It works every time.

When people cease to have worries and concerns, they will die of excess satisfaction. Habit, with its limitations, is the most palatable form of satisfaction any human can handle. And don't forget: "perfection" is nothing more than satisfaction.

My Enemy

I have enemies. My enemies are those who impair my happiness and contentment, in whatever manner, by whatever means, and for whatever their reasons. I don't care whether they are black, brown, yellow or white; whether they are Jew, Christian, Muslim or Buddhist.

My enemy has made it impossible for me to buy an ice cream cone for a nickel, a home for ten thousand dollars, a new car for under one thousand dollars, and a fine pair of shoes for under ten.

"Inflation," you tell me. "Increased labor costs. The need for higher wages."

"Greed," I say.

My enemy has stolen my home from me, legally, in a court of law. My enemy has blocked my driveway. My enemy has vandalized my car. My enemy has made it impossible for me to purchase a bit of nostalgia that no one else wants, unless I am willing to pay an exorbitant price.

On the other hand, my enemy is not the disc jockey in the radio studio who plays music abrasive to my ear. Nor is my enemy the TV program director who would present the same kind of fare, no matter what. Popular entertainments have always been slanted to the simplest mentality. I need not participate in them, for they can be turned off. You say, "You are wrong; they promote what you call your enemy—greed and inflation." Yes, they do, but I do not respond. I do not help to make it so. It is the vast, unthinking public which does. It is they who support and escalate inflation, because their brains are too feeble and shortsighted to consider the effects of their greed to make more money. "But we have to live," they wail. "It's the high cost of living." I did not increase the cost of living, for them or anyone else. My wants and needs have always been within my grasp. I did not raise the price of copper or plastics, necessitating increased production costs. Why should I be penalized for it?

I do not worry about crime in the streets. I can pull a trigger. But I can't make the man sell me an ice cream cone for a nickel.

Don't actively protest an impersonal war waged by people who have a history of conflict. Don't bomb abortion clinics unless you happen to need one, and they won't take you. Then, bombs away! Men should bomb lawyers offices if they are being personally sued for everything they have worked for. My point is, select your enemy with the same logic and reason that you would use in selecting a friend. Or an appliance. Or a book. With discrimination and an eye towards your own personal involvement.

My enemies make my life less enriched and more complicated. That depletes me. It bothers me that I cannot buy a comic book for a dime anymore. I was neither appalled nor surprised when James Huberty shot up the McDonald's because the ice cream machine was still broken. If there is a lesson to be learned there, it is this: If you're going to charge over a nickel for an ice cream cone, you'd better give special service. More than most, Huberty was a qualified activist: one who performs acts of terrorism against persons or agencies having nothing to do with any personal involvement.

Who is responsible for the crimes against me? Not blacks, Latinos, or Jews, but those who support the ultimate demands of greed. The stupid, myopic public who is so easily duped into focusing on manufactured misdirection enemies, rather than those who really rob them.

The Satanic Murderer

The mind of the murderer has been studied and analyzed ever since murder was considered a social aberration. Despite the intensity of the crime itself and an impressive parade of scholars, little has been discovered beyond certain clichéd hypotheses and presuppositions. As technology advances, new methods of detection are employed. As social climates change, new and consuming interest in the topic presents itself. Most technical and scientific questions can be answered, despite an ongoing wonder at an obsessive interest in "true crime." If more murders are solved, it is certainly because of technological advances rather than better detective work. There is more capable equipment, but fewer capable detectives. A professional "psychic" might be employed to offer an intuitive hunch that the most defective detective would likely have considered in the old days of "scientific crime detection" and "blue sense." Political correctness has negated an emphasis on "typing" people. Hence, the over mind, the zeitgeist, has filtered down to the investigator, who in turn, lacks crucial abilities. Since Lombroso's "criminal type" was discredited, the baby has been thrown out with the bath water. If any generalizations are to be made (and many have been), they dwell upon the childhood traumas and tribulations of the murderer and the sexual substitution and/or gratification in the act itself.

Too little has been studied about the victim type: the habitual maladroit who is waiting for an executioner. Or having found one, the unlimited desperation to win the jackpot of death. Too little has been written of the small, insignificant, ordinary people whose dull lives are enlivened by murder, and who themselves wait out their remaining days in frenetic complacency without the comparative thrill of getting themselves killed.

The primary motives for murder remain: passion, profit, revenge. But look: a new constellation appears. The cosmology of Satanism dictates that established Judeo-Christian standards be reevaluated on all levels and in all areas. Values of right and wrong can no longer be equated with arbitrary, yet increasingly debatable standards of "good and evil." Even though human nature remains unchanged, causal options do. A man may no longer be moved to cruelty to horses because of being thrown by them on several occasions. Now, the same kind of fellow, after suffering a succession of automobile injuries, might feel a pathological hatred for motor cars. Transference takes more forms than limited imaginations can detect.

If the severest obstacle in the detection of murder is a limited imagination, the next in line is *too much* imagination, i.e., a need to fictionalize to the point of hysteria. We have observed how vicarious conjecture has placed Satanic criminals, like McCarthy-era communists, under every bed—including killers who can conveniently be labeled "Satanic," though their only connection is a copy of *The Satanic Bible.* Such selective flights of fancy eliminate all reference to Christian murders in hotel rooms wherein rests a Gideon *Bible.* This is not to imply that there are no Satanic murders. If gross convenient ignorance precludes an accurate evaluation of a truly Satanic murder, there is no way of knowing how many otherwise "normal" murders are in reality, Satanic.

The only yardstick with which to evaluate the mind of a murderer are findings provided by those who have been apprehended. No one studies those who have not been caught....

THE LIARS CLUB

I'm one helluva liar. Most of my adult life, I've been accused of being a charlatan, a phony, an impostor. I guess that makes me about as close to what the Devil's supposed to be, as anyone.

It's true.

I lie constantly, incessantly.

Because I lie so often, I'd *really* be full of shit if I didn't keep my mouth shut and my bowels open.

I say "keep my *mouth* shut"—I want to emphasize that part, because that is the organ from whence my most incurable lies emanate. I would have made a good PR man, because my most flagrant lies are to other people, about themselves. If the Devil is a flatterer, I do my job well.

My lies are not about myself. My accusers and detractors go to great lengths to show that they are. They miss the entire show while concentrating on the reflection. I serve as a projection of their own Walter Mitty lives of inconsequence. I allow them the luxury of character inversion. Those who are first to accuse me of falsification are themselves living examples of fakery incarnate. Some even know it.

I only lie about myself when I know that I'm fulfilling another's expectations. On that score, what they see is what they get. I really don't have to lie. I must brag that I am the real thing, the real McCoy, the one of a kind genuine article. But my listener, my audience—now that's a different story.

I am the worst kind of rascal, for I flatter up like nobody's business. I am an unwilling, habitual practitioner of what Gypsies call "lavengro." It is the art of telling people what they want most to hear, and the fortune teller's stock and trade. A therapist would call it "supportive" and note that it reinforces another's self-esteem. The lower one's self-esteem, the more valuable and effective it is.

Oh, how I lie! If a fellow be a churlish lout, I tell him how sensitive and discriminating he is. If a girl is so ugly that she must sneak up on a glass of water, I allude to her great beauty. If one's performance is medicore at best, I applaud his great talent. I praise the skinflint on his generosity and the hysteric on his levelheaded judiciousness. And it makes them all feel good.

Occasionally, my praise is genuine. The trouble with that is, those with the most to offer are usually their own severest critics, so I make them feel a little bit better, but not really good. The worst soar, at least temporarily. They're always the first to label me a phony and a charlatan. I wonder why.

My own achievements are demonstrable. My detractors cannot demonstrate anything of real or lasting value. If they are "writers," they fill many pages, but say very little. If they are "musicians," they equate loudness with talent. If they are "glamorous," the labels on their clothes are what make them so.

If I should ever meet you, don't believe a word of what I say— about you.

THE SNEEZE

Little, if anything, has been written on the therapeutic value of volitional sneezing. It has been acknowledged that sneezing is, like yawning, scratching, and stretching, an involuntary act. More than any other natural function, a sneeze approximates an orgasm. It brings with it release, at least temporary. It, like orgasm, has been likened by metaphysicians to a mini-death. Superstition is rife with the symbolism of the sneeze, ranging in meaning from "a sneeze lets the demons in and must be immediately acknowledged as such" (God bless you!)—to the other extreme, "a sneeze purges the demons within." (God bless you!) Even the number of sneezes counts for something; one being a warning, two being a danger, and three being safe.

Getting back to the therapeutic value of a sneeze: Given that a sneeze is a miniature orgasm or death throe; it is easier, quicker, and less messy to sneeze than to have an orgasm. It is surely easier and less complicated to sneeze, than to die. It has been well established that an orgasm is beneficial for many reasons. It has also been established that death, aside from being final and permanent, eases and solves all pressures and problems.

To sneeze is to scratch an itch. It is only annoying when it reaches a frequency which becomes uncomfortable, such as when provoked by hay fever, allergy, flu, colds, etc. When a sneeze appears not to be necessary, it is at its therapeutic best. The release accorded by a sneeze goes far beyond the area most obviously affected, i.e., the nose. *Like an orgasm, it is profound in its totality.*

In order to produce a therapeutic sneeze, as opposed to an involuntary one, certain tricks must be employed. Therapeutic sneezing is like masturbation, in that it is a conscious act designed to gratify. It's easy to trick oneself, and it's easy to produce a sneeze using physical and psychological tricks.

Physical manipulation is almost always necessary. The fine hairs of the nostrils responsible for detecting and responding to odors and other subtle stimuli must be artificially manipulated. Sniffing pepper or snuff would fall into this category, and for some it may suffice. Joke-shop "sneezing powder" is simply such an irritant. A safe foreign object inserted into a nostril will yield the same results, if used as a tickler. A stripped-down Q-Tip is ideal. The only problem inherent in artificially-induced sneezing is *desensitization.* It is very much like overcoming the gag reflex when learning the art of sword swallowing. Eventually, the nostrils become desensitized until no amount of poking or tickling will achieve the desired result: an involuntary sneeze.

There is, not surprisingly, the equivalent of a female "G spot" within the nostril. With time, care, and psychological help, this "S spot" can be isolated, and subsequently stimulated to a healthy sneeze.

An important consideration is the psychological aspect of volitional sneezing. As an aid to production, it helps to be able to mentally fixate on something relevant to a sneeze. Contagion is a prime factor in yawning, laughter, boredom, itching, etc. Likewise, contagion can be a powerful ally to a volitional sneeze.

A personal example was my emerging awareness of the therapeutic value of a sneeze brought about as a sexual adjunct—what could be stronger? A certain young lady whom I found sexually stimulating was afflicted with a lifelong type of incontinence which, among other precipitators, was brought about by sneezing. Every time she sneezed, she involuntarily wet her panties—which, to my jaded tastes, was exceptionally stimulating. It may have distressed *her,* but it excited *me.* In fact, it became so indelibly etched into my libido that I had no trouble bridging the gap and defining it as a vicarious but effective substitute for Reich's *Function of the Orgasm.* The exhilaration obtained from seeing the results of my friend's sneezes created a mental image so strong as to contagiously make me seek the same relief, sans incontinence. The sight of her performance accompanied by a tickle of my own nostril, could make me sneeze in a manner that relaxed and energized my entire being.

Unfortunately, there is a sad outcome to what had been a foolproof and completely gratifying form of sneeze therapy. When the young lady realized the benefits *I* was getting from her dilemma—the approval and encouragement I made clear—she was miraculously "cured," and no matter how much she sneezed, she emerged a very proper and very dry young lady.

Souⁿd Retreat

Why do some celebrities retreat from public view beyond a certain point in their lives, while others remain—only to die untimely deaths? Elvis Presley, Marilyn Monroe, and others refused to remove themselves from the public which fed upon them. Others, like Marlene Dietrich, Kim Novak, and Joe DiMaggio voluntarily isolate themselves and live out their lives in hiding. Still others *tried* to remove themselves from the curse of public dependency but somehow suffered the residue of responsibility—the iconographic focus was too much for them. Despite their attempts to put a wall between themselves and the parasitic public, they still succumbed. Among them were Howard Hughes, Ty Cobb, Rudy Vallee, and Jayne Mansfield. The latter grouping revealed just enough of themselves and their disdain for the public to make themselves unloved, though still needed. They were controversial but necessary.

The public feeds off of their leaders. The most beloved leader is constantly depleted by a negative discharge his constituents' dependency maintains. No matter their well wishes; they might just as well be curses. The intensity of the public's focus is all that matters. It depletes, drains, and—if protective measures are not taken—destroys.

The audience—the public—is a dependent organism. Their very

lack of consequence makes them parasitic to their leaders. They really contribute nothing, so all they can do is drain. Sure, token roles of varying importance are bestowed upon them. The only real loser is still the symbolic figure at the end of the line. It may be said that the leader gains his strength from that very human mass which drains him—that it is a reciprocal thing. It is not, nor can it ever be. The sheer weight of public focus—the magnitude of its psychic dependency—is so overwhelming as to take its toll on a leader. Any leader's survival is in direct proportion to his ability to secretly remove himself from the effects of his fans. Though *their* concern may be unrelenting, the leader must do everything within his power to depersonalize himself from them.

How does a symbolic leader save himself from the fame that curses? Isolation and reclusiveness are important. Stay out of the marketplace. An ambivalence to current trends and affairs further draws a barrier. Above all, a hedonistic lack of schedule, commitment, and responsibility is the strongest weapon towards purely personal pacing. One might liken it to an exotic animal in captivity—one who is dependent upon a kind and understanding keeper. Or a small child whose parents derive infinite pleasure from its antics—its very presence—and provide for its day to day needs. In short: the great leader must "reduce" himself to something less than an adult human being. Only through rejection of his own sophisticated humanness can he maintain a tranquillity necessary to his continuance. He must discard all societal rules and regulations. He must live as though there were no clocks, no calendars, and subsequently, no appointments to be met. He must withdraw himself from the affairs and measurements of men, and become as hedonistic as the staunchest moralist (or faddist) is not. It is humanity that will surely kill him if allowed. Humanity has murdered every god it has created—except one. The Evil One. The One who endures and prevails.

What's New?

Most people die from newness. Contrary to the accepted premise of staying young by keeping up on things, newness is a devastating, death-dealing state. Constantly changing standards invalidate life-maintaining *stasis.* The only way you can get old is by exposure to the new. Each fresh excursion into the contemporary negates that, which if fiercely retained, would continue to provide an ageless state of limbo. If there is no present to involuntarily match the past against, the past *remains the present.* And you remain the *past present,* or, like a vampire, the way you were in your prime.

Many examples have been shown. *After Many a Summer Dies the Swan, Corridor of Mirrors, She, Lost Horizon.* What is thought to be "rarefied air" within which the ageless dwell is but a metaphor for "time standing still."

The pollution of the present is literally deadly poison. Whenever possible, an emissary or liaison must be employed to bring supplies in from the outside world and negotiate business. A seemingly harmless occasional trip outside can cause debilitating radiation sickness, necessitating actual recuperation. Again, the metaphor of the ageless one melting away after leaving its rarefied environment—sometimes a short passage through a cleft in a mountain pass—has great validity.

I have personally known individuals who implemented the formula with admirable success. They only succumbed when they were forced to make regular forays into the world, thus suffering the ensuing debilitation. Two examples were Dr. Nixon and Samson de Brier. Had they had less contact with the outside world and been allowed to exist totally within the confines of their idealized worlds, they might have lived much longer. One thing is certain: like Dorian Gray, neither *appeared* much older than when he was significantly younger. Strange, how these types never really look as young as they really are in their youth, either. When Dr. Nixon was in his 20s, he appeared to be in his 40s When in his 60s, he appeared to be in his 40s.

It helps to avoid seeing people. The old ones are dull, their meaningful memories divested and replaced with contemporary pap; and physically ugly. The young ones are mentally impoverished, illiterate, and "Typhoid Marys" of contemporary contagion. Both are cultural and aesthetic saboteurs.

Attempts to "enlighten" young persons are noble but depleting. The time and energy spent in attempts to alter the effects of contemporization only subject the bestower of life to the contagion of transitory values. Susceptibility is greater than immunization. If you attempt to provide others with antibodies against the disease of newness, you are fighting the odds. The older a person is, the more important *conservation of energy* becomes.

What about immunity? What does one do to protect oneself if forced into the outside world? The answer is to treat it as any other form of deadly radiation. Heavily tinted glasses turn day into night. Ear plugs can help. When a seemingly deaf Satanist was loudly asked, "Hard of hearing?" he replied, "No—just tired of listening." I have known old-timers who literally turn down their hearing aids. Some have more trouble "shutting down" than do others. That's why it's best to play it safe and wear a gas mask.

It is a misnomer to assume that one must "live in the past." Living in the past is not enough. It becomes a random hodgepodge of stylistic approaches, none of which is a genuine time warp of sufficient emotional intensity. Far preferable to live in a past; an era embraced because it, more than any other, represents one's best interests and most vital responses.

If you must know what's going on in the outside world, have a liaison fill you in on only what you need to know. If you are a true candidate for agelessness, there won't be much you will *care* to know.

A helpful exercise is to keep up on the news—the news, that is, of the time frame you exist within. Keep periodicals at hand to reinforce what's happening in the world. This may entail acquiring a collection of vintage newspapers and magazines, popular books of the period, indigenous musical recordings, etc. If you feel in the least deprived of outside stimulation, the lifestyle is not for you.

Clothing of the period must be as rigidly maintained as a Japanese feudal household. Instead of all shoes being removed at the door, suitable attire must be worn in your presence at all times. Nothing shatters the life-sustaining stasis of a time warp more than the counter-visuals of contemporary fashion. Loose fitting smocks may be provided at the door, if necessary. (Disney World has already implemented this device in its total environments.) This will allow you to imagine your occasional mandatory guests as monks from some compatible religious order—and treat them accordingly.

Conversation must be without any reference to present conditions. It helps to employ the vernacular of the chosen period. Rather than letting yourself "roll with the punches," pretend that you don't quite understand what your guest is saying, if his speech pattern is invasive. Better to be thought eccentric and difficult to deal with. At best, our visitor will honor your environment with a conducive speech pattern. At worst, he will leave and not return.

Genuineness and authenticity of artifacts is less important than *effect.* If ersatz materials and modern reproductive techniques produce a convincingly realistic time warp, it matters little that a book is not an original edition, but a replica. What is important is the content. The fact that you are reading a book that *looks* like an old copy of *Main Street,* and *is* that very story, places you within the time frame of your vital survival. Just make sure you tear out the omnipresent contemporary postcard insert offering other books in the "Classic Editions" series.

Get the idea?

Iꞃferiorism

I first noticed it when automobiles appeared on which the trim that was usually chrome was now painted to match the color of the car's body. It seemed especially desirable on red, black, or white vehicles. I had heard that chromium had become scarce and costly due to a Soviet near-monopoly on it, and that's why American cars were using extreme reversals of what had been traditional use of chrome trim. The use of chromium had reached its point of critical mass in the late 60s, following an increasingly flagrant display throughout the 50s. The new "clean look" took hold by the late 80s, and at that decade's end, there was hardly a single model which didn't have painted trim. It was expected, and no one felt deprived of chrome trim and bumpers. After all, aren't plastic bumpers safer? But I have belabored my point.

For years, the only cars that had painted trim and bumpers were the stripped down "economy" models, purchased for utilitarian use by farmers, frugal Scotsmen, or other taciturn Percy Kilbride types. When the second world war came along, the few cars made available had austere painted trim, in order to "conserve chromium for the war effort," whatever that meant. Other than the two examples I've mentioned, the more chrome a car displayed, the higher the status, with the only exception being the 1936–37 Cord, now considered a half-century ahead of its time. Objectively, the Cord's actual design did not lend itself to much trim of any sort. The truly advanced twist of the Cord was that it was made with extremely tight production costs, so a design had to be created which would look expensive but cost a minimum to produce.

After the war, in 1946, a new school of modification came, producing both the hot rod and the dechromed, lowered custom car. Of course, neither was taken seriously by mature people, and their only drivers were wild-eyed marginal types, usually youthful and invariably delinquent. The mainstream still demanded—and received—lots of chrome trim. Then came the great invocation of inferiorism.

Inferiorism is the foisting of the undesirable in any form, upon a public which not only accepts the inferior, but transmutes it into the most desirable.

It comes in all manner. Clothing that once would be relegated to the prison work farm, clown alley, or skid row, becomes not only the most fashionable, but the most costly to purchase. I need not cite the elements of what has been termed "poverty chic." The more worn, ragged, ill-fitting, and "stressed," the better. And the higher the cost, the more fashionable.

Foods which were once inexpensive alternatives to costlier dining—Chinese, Mexican, East Indian, Italian, rural American (chicken, ribs, etc.)—have attained gourmet status and prices. A flagrant example of inferiorism is pizza. It was once an economy dish, like Chinese and Mexican food, that could provide a low budget eating experience in an ethnic, stimulating setting. Now, it has risen in cost to meet all other dining experiences, and why? Because it got respectable. Most good pizza costs a premium—on a par with a steak dinner. But wait— did I say *good* pizza? Thick, doughy, half-baked pizza is being served up as "Sicilian" and superior to the wafer-thin stuff which conscientious Sicilian pizza makers pridefully spun in midair. Recent "authentic deep dish pizza" is only "authentic" to suburban American housing tracts. Kids were raised on woefully inadequate attempts to create "homemade" pizza, as opposed to the frozen variety, which is actually much better. So where does the lousy stuff wind up? At "gourmet" pizza parlors for higher prices.

Inferiorism is an inevitable result of the "less is more" school of thought and merchandising. All is not lost though. I foresee, as a natural consequence, a return to flagrant and ostentatious alternatives. Already, "sleaze" and "white trash" looks are becoming popular. A "slut look" for women and "gangster style" formality for men is emerging. The new formalism will place classiness above cleanliness, and soiled suits above freshly laundered rags. More young people than ever are seeking an anti-yuppie, anti-hippie image. Cars with tail fins and lots of chrome are becoming more desirable than they ever were when new. A new youth is emerging with a Satanic aesthetic. Lyrical music is returning, this time with more vigor than ever. The painstakingly representational art of Joe Coleman, Robert Williams, and Coop is replacing abstractionist swill and crudely inept ethno/primitive "culture." It will take more than a Warhol enlargement of a soup can to earn accolades for artistic expression.

Once inferiorism is discerned and dissected, there's no turning back. True to Luciferian tradition, enlightenment often arrives only through the opportunity for comparisons to be drawn. The antidote to inferiorism is renewed—or fresh—exposure to that which has been conveniently replaced; forgotten by some, but never even encountered by most.

Revolutions happen when sufficient amounts of humans realize that they have been "took in." Inferiorism glorifies whatever will provide the highest profit from the least investment, whether in objects, services, or human beings.

THE DEATH OF FASHION

Judeo-Christianity and fashion are inseparable. Both are the great enemies of progress beyond the 20th century. There are direct parallels:

Satan is the patron of all that is unfashionable. All his works can be reduced to that simple single definition of "Evil." Scientific advancement is delayed and curtailed by both. "New and improved" is a construct of greedy merchants who prey upon man's carefully nurtured insecurities and dissatisfaction. The arbiters of fashion are in the business of obsolescence. So is science and technology. They differ in that science can be used to build a better world, while fashion renders the scientist unfashionable. The great enemy Fashion impedes even the most revolutionary scientific advance. Eliminate the existence of fashion within the scientific community, and watch it flourish with new approaches.

Fashion, like Christianity, is a death cult. Both create dissatisfaction, insecurity and uncertainty silenced only by death. Fashion, like its Christian ally, could only work with herd humans—those who can only feel temporary security in group acceptance. I have already made my statement regarding ECI and its relationship to longevity. The most naturally conservative person could go about his business much better without concern for fashion.

Futurists have predicted an Orwellian kind of universal garment. Like parochial school uniforms, priority would be placed on achievement rather than fashion. In theory, that is sound because fashion has no place where progress is concerned. How ironic that only within the strictest religious environments is there escape from fashion. Quakers, Shakers, Mennonites, Hassidim, Hindi, etc. are exempt. The only problem I see with that is that futurists are by nature leptosomes to whom sexual allure and gender differentiation have low priority. Their aesthetic ideal is a unisex Spandex jumpsuit. Their motives are honorable, but their libidos weak.

Satanism as a mass movement can maintain a Pythagorean standard—a Golden Mean—of aesthetic classicism that could last for a millennium.

I am the arbiter of that aesthetic. It celebrates a distinct difference between genders, encouraging heterosexual continuance of the race, yet devoid of changing fashion. Birth control and eugenics must be dealt with, independent of aesthetic.

Inasmuch as all standards of all religions are by decree, I place myself among the priests and rabbins who proclaim aesthetic standards. My qualification for the establishment of a Satanic aesthetic is my ability to produce and perform in that capacity. Let he who would challenge me produce his superiority in those realms.

Are Mormon missionaries, Jesuit priests, Rabbinical scholars, Mennonites, and Quakers—like their Roman Lictor predecessors—agents of Satan because they eschew fashion and wear black?

A young boy watched as a nun waited to cross a busy street. Taking her arm, he held his other up to stop traffic. They reached the opposite side of the street safely. When the nun thanked him profusely for his assistance, the boy responded: "That's OK, lady. Any friend of Zorro is a friend of mine!"

Identifiable Aesthetic Standards of Satanism

The softening-up process has set the stage. "Pre-stressed," "stonewashed," and "tie dyed" garments have negated a need for a new and unused appearance. It's now possible to wear clothes with snags, runs, rips, gaps, tears, discoloration, stains, moth holes, and other imperfections. Clothing may be too tight or too loose. Condition is unimportant. Overall imagery is.

Satanic style is based on the questionable, if not unacceptable. If females dress like archetypical whores and males like archetypical villains, the Satanic, the dark side, is celebrated. In response to the question, "What happens when everyone dresses like that?" the answer is, "They never will." Like nuns and Quakers, Satanic men and women will be recognized by their distinctive garb. However seedy their raiment might be, it adheres to classic Pythagorean form. Because of that, it has insidious appeal in that it invites others to slip into Satanism as they would slip into its clothing or partake of its other aesthetic standards. It is the tail wagging the dog; a change in personality by changing one's handwriting.

Hardware (automobiles, equipment, etc.) reclaims masculine form long rejected as "phallic." "Muscle" equates to "male" in our world. Androgyny is recognized as per *The Satanic Witch,* not as a visual dilemma. If a female Satanist wishes to dress as a man, she should do it with conviction and completion, cropping her hair, lowering her voice, building up muscles, and pasting on beard or moustache. She should present herself as male in every way and by any means possible.

Likewise, a male who wishes to present a female aesthetic image should become a completely honest TV or transsexual. Difference and contrast are Satanic. Homogenization is not. There is no place for visually-mixed gender identification in our world, unless displayed by hermaphroditism in a side show.

Male and female sexual differentiation and allure reached its Golden Mean in the mid-20th century, i.e. post-Victorian and pre-unisex. Within the religion of Satanism male and female elements are equally important in the truest sense.

Satanic Weddings:
Why I Don't Perform Them

I don't perform Satanic weddings for the same reason I would hesitate to be a party to my own. In the past, the wedding ceremony was a viable extension of other human activities. Within the context of then-existing standards it did more than serve a purpose; it was an essential part of "normal" life.

The first and most important reason for marriage was sex. It was the only way millions of people could indulge themselves without guilt. Christianity had placed sin on a pedestal from which religious sanction alone could amend it. Marriage was just such an amendment. That's why people got married. They had either hot nuts or hot pants. Love? Sure. The most intense feelings of love were not *incompatible* with marriage. After all, to a feminine mystique, love and sex are inexorably intertwined. My point is that love and marriage translated meant love and sex. Like the analogy of the square and the rectangle, one could experience love with or without marriage; but no marriage, no sex.

Of course, the sexual validation provided by a marriage license was only the beginning. It inspired servicemen on leave to marry girls they had known for two hours. It also resulted in alarming spousal obsolescence, with divorces and annulments filed with the rapidity of weddings. Even then, the quickest, most perfunctory vows often resulted in the longest marriages. Those that survived were obviously based on more than religious sanction. Still, many elaborate church weddings and lavish traditional ceremonies produced long marriages, though fear of ostracism from church or God insured most. Divorce was a sin as devastating as sex without marriage.

The Bigger The Wedding, The Shorter The Marriage

The evidence against formal weddings and officially sanctioned marriages is formidable:

In a world devoid of commitments—a severely imposed disposable society—to memorialize anything is disquieting. It violates the comforting habits of freedom from restraints, upward mobility, "new and improved" change, informality, and instant (and temporal) gratification.

A "return to traditional values" in an Orwellian society only means that a wedding ceremony, and formalized marriage itself, is a charming and quaint act of protest. The frame becomes more important than the picture. At one time the frame sanctioned and validated the picture. Often now, there is not even a picture—just an empty frame.

Because of universal depersonalization and dependency on technology, true love is rare enough—with or without marriage. Real love, despite party line counsel to the contrary, is permeated with dependency, as well it should be. It should therefore come as no surprise that dependency upon the system and its non-human servitors has replaced dependency upon mates. One falls in love and cohabitates with his or her computer.

Marriage imposes rules where none are wanted. An "ideal" marriage is a non-marriage where no rules apply and both parties are "free" to go their own ways. There is nothing wrong with that. But why call it marriage? Why formalize what is intended as informal? Does not the stigma assumed by formalization place greater stress upon an already tenuous responsibility?

Finery for Slobs

The very formality of a wedding strains the informality which is sure to follow. The gulf is vast. In the past, participants and guests at a formal wedding dressed up as much or more than when going to church or to the movies or to the state fair. The formality of a wedding did not contrast to the point of discomfort. Now, the strained formality of a wedding is glaringly conducive to a comfortable return to jeans and t-shirts—until the next wedding (or funeral).

An elaborate and formal wedding in an informal world carries a terrifying implication of future or *ongoing* formalism. The stage has been set. The comfortable (and necessary) informality which is sure to follow can, and does, turn *casuality* into *casualty.*

Within *existing*—not traditional—context, elaborate weddings condemn even the most potentially productive unions to failure. I haven't lost a bet in 25 years predicting the short-term results of big weddings.

Satanic Marriages to Demon Lovers

The only viable wedding in an irresponsible and informal world is a Satanic one—to a demon spouse.

The more humans fail to think, feel, respond; the greater the appeal, the greater the need for an idealized mate. A frustrating search—a trial and error approach—produces lots of trials, plenty of errors, and ends in worse frustration then ever.

Even in an idealized setting, time frame, and environment, it's still hard to find the right mate. It is easier to select the right mate for one-self from the most readily available stock: one's own mind.

Start small. If you can't conjure up a satisfactory demon lover, you can never hope to even approach the real thing. Only if and when you can be satisfied with an image (remember, unapproved images are prohibited by Holy writ) can you attract an actualization.

One of the strongest arguments against masturbation advanced by "experts" was its deleterious effect on the attainment of a real flesh and blood relationship. It was claimed that if you masturbated to sat-isfaction, you'd get into a habit which would negate any need for the real thing. In other words, you'd wind up happier with a first-rate fantasy than a third-rate partner. Of course, it wasn't exactly put in those terms; but in a contemporary way, that argument against mas-turbation becomes a fine case *for* it. As a sage once declared, "I'm married to my right hand."

As sanctioned marriages and formal weddings became less pro-ductive, it occurred to me that there was really nothing so much wrong with the ceremony and institution. It was the principal charac-ters involved. The one-way streets of love became devoid of destina-tion. It wasn't so much that one person was the lover and the other the love object. The problem always seemed to be in the love object. Decidedly inferior merchandise.

A solution? Discover or create a demon spouse, using available ideals. Then, have as big a Satanic wedding as you please. Your mar-riage will last as long as you want it to, and you'll never be disap-pointed. Come to think of it, that's the only kind of wedding I'd per-form, in my present capacity.

THE SONG OF THE SHIELD

I furtively glance up a skirt...
Some longed-for glimpse of secret sights I seek.
And by and by my glance returns its answer:
I spy no hint of underpants or
Stocking top.
But in their stead, proud panty hose
Perfumed by strong astringent soap and
Reeking of celibacy.

If perchance, I might see pants
Where panties should be found,
I'll ponder what delights repose
Within the silken mound.

But silk no more is used to spin
The covering, so sleek, so thin.
Nor rayon, or most any stuff
Condemned to keep the moisture in.

Not even nylon, on its own, is safe enough to wear.
For foulness dwells within the crease
Between the lumpy thighs.
A fetid stench assails the air
And rancid vapors scorch their eyes.

Oh, panty shield, oh panty shield...
Thank God you were invented!
You keep the ladies fresh and dry
And sterile, safe, and sanitized,
To ply their charms contentedly
Without the terror of a blush
That comes from a foul telltale rush of
Dread excess lubricity.

What if, with luck,
Good fortune smiled upon me?
That I might see
Above a knee
A thigh encased in perfidy
And covered not
By denim, Lycra, Spandex,
Binding most acceptably,
Concealing most effectively;
Ascending to a non-existent waist.

Just let me glimpse
A stocking top with
Garters fastened,
Reaching up and over thighs
All milky white
With cellulite.
Anticipation reigns supreme.

That I might be so fortunate
That I might yield to speculate
What I might do to violate
The sanctity of crotch revealed;
Stained and sodden,

So tantalizingly concealed
Within those naked, sweaty inner thighs.

But I can only fantasize, for
Nowhere in this world, it seems,
My childhood joys and youthful lusts
Can replicate themselves, and
I must learn to be turned on, and
Randy at the sight of
Birkenstocks and leotards;
The cloying smell of sexy gel,
Adroitly blended with a scent of
Inoffensive anti-perspirant.

No more, for me,
Above the knees lies ecstasy
Unhampered by propriety
So false, so modest, and so clean, that
By comparison, the
Nuns of old
Were harlots.

Take me back in space and time
Where I can smell a
Woman's smell
To lead me down the spoor.
Where gals could be unladylike,
While feminine and pure.
When sweaty thighs were lusty thighs and
Women weren't dry;
And pulchritude could oft be seen in every woman's eyes.

Going even further back;
The rut, the syrinx shrill;
The stomping of the cloven hooves
While nymphs and pards quadrilled
And in the glade, the Host forbade that
Never in some future place,
His own would even tolerate a race of
Beings, devolved to such disgrace
That the sounds of the rut would be replaced by the
Crinkling plastic of a
Sterile,
Sanitary,
Moisture free,
Deodorized
Panty shield.

L'Envoi

THE ~~POLICEMAN~~ LAWYER
IS YOUR FRIEND

$\bigodot$nce upon a time, children of law-abiding parents were taught that despite an authoritarian image, the policeman was a friend, primarily concerned with the keeping of order and the protection of citizens. Occasionally, due to anomalous circumstances, that benign image was altered and one became a cop-hater. In other words, the role of policeman went the way of Heroes, Villains, and Fools. The prime generalization was heroic. The secondary, as applied to the bullying and corrupt cop—villainous. The third, serving as underlying comic relief, was the Keystone Cop, the dumb flatfoot, the defective detective.

Since the advent of politically correct liberal fascism, policemen are not the same. They are visible reminders that there is still order. They are token icons wearing uniforms and driving vehicles which stand out from the rest. They are respected, if for no other reason, because they can legally carry guns. No one wants to get shot. Their cars can go through red lights and park anywhere. They can eat vast amounts of free doughnuts and speak to any pretty girl they choose. All this, because of past conditioning as authority figures. Yet their hands are bound. They can be sued. Their authority ends on the street. It goes no further. They are little more than privileged citizens who still must work a regular shift and act as part of a team. Unless they solve an unsolvable crime, they will have to consume many doughnuts at one sitting to qualify for *Guinness*. They can wear a star, but they can never be one.

If a policeman's lot is not a happy one, that is not the case with attorneys. They can get away with just about anything. And get paid for it.

But let's not jump to conclusions. The lawyer is our friend. He can, and has, replaced the cop. An old-time cop could pinch either an apple from a vendor's cart or a baby on the cheek—or maybe even the nursemaid's bottom. But a cop can no longer indulge in such diversion, for the lawyer has power over him. Now that everyone is accounted for by computerized checkout, our old time cop would die lousy. If he was spotted during the act of stealing the fruit man's apple he would, upon identification, be served with papers attesting to the fact that he willfully, and with malice, did contaminate certain other fruits while engaging in the selection of that which he subsequently misappropriated. The infant in the perambulator would have been traumatically abused, suffering contusions of the cheek and permanent impairment of the facial muscles. As for the nursemaid: sexual assault on the part of a trusted public servant is not to be trifled with. The Court takes a dim view of police officers who, in the line of duty, attempt to rape women—especially those overseeing the safety of babies and small children.

Alas, the unfortunate outcome of the aforementioned incidents would certainly result in the offending officer's discharge from duty, thereby disqualifying him from any benefits upon his retirement two years later. His paid-for home would be sold to settle, with minimal satisfaction, the awards granted by the Court to the lawyers, the fruit merchant, the infant's parents, and the emotionally scarred nursemaid. Our policeman's family—wife, children and grandchildren—burdened with shame, have left and disowned him, and having taken up residence in another city, changed their surname. The ex-policeman, working incognito as a night watchman in a sausage warehouse, has only baloney for company and bratwurst for solace.

SAFE PLACES AND RATS NESTS

Have you ever relocated an item of importance to a "safe place," only to be unable to henceforth find it? For example: an important and frequently consulted book is kept in a box with discarded clothes and a stack of inconsequential magazines. You realize, after removing and replacing the book numerous times, that it is in a place unsuited for its storage. You decide to put the book where it will be better protected and more readily available. After a couple of months, you need the book. You cannot remember where you put it. You can go right to the carton where the book had carelessly lain ever since its purchase, but try as you might, you've completely forgotten where its new "safe place" is.

A familiar scenario, but explainable.

Much as we'd like to believe in the triumph of order over chaos, we seem to lose out to disorder every time. Not really, though. There is actually more order, but of a different sort, when your misplaced item is in its unsafe and unsuitable storage space.

It is easier to remember anything by way of time rather than distance. We think in terms of how long it takes us to drive to a certain place, rather than how many actual miles away it is or where it lies geographically. We remember things relative to a particular time frame. Einstein realized the relevance of time and space. Quite simply, you originally placed your book where you could always find it in a place relevant to the *time it was purchased.* Such chronological filing systems may look like a rat's nest, but will unerringly yield what you seek. After a few removals and replacements, any item's location becomes indelibly remembered. The worst thing you can do is remove and relocate such an item to a "more suitable place." It's a sure way to lose it—to throw it out of orbit—until it's accidentally stumbled upon, invariably at some date in the distant future and when there is no immediate need for it.

Habit dies hard, and habit is maintained by the comforting principle of predictability. That's another reason why nothing should ever be relocated to a "safe place." Any attempt to find an article which has been relocated after a long time in the same place constitutes a significant change of habit. After being accustomed to being able to find a particular item "with your eyes shut," you not only must open both eyes, but jam your brain trying to figure out where its new "safe place" is.

On a larger scale, when one moves to a new and "improved" location and things start to go wrong, the same old principle applies. Crummy as the old location may have been, it was familiar and therefore predictable. It may have been, by my first premise, blessed with enough benign or pleasant chronological events to maintain a comfortable semblance of order. When the feeling of needing to "live better" starts to nag, relocation to a "safer" place seems the logical answer. Then, once things are done "right," the trouble really begins.

How does one beat the odds? You can't. You can live by additive synthesis, acquiring newly chronicled items, but the old must not be relocated. Discarded? Yes. Stored away? Yes. But *never* placed in a more suitable location for ready accessibility. The best kept belongings are those kept in cartons, bags, stacks, and other unlikely places. If you want an orderly *and* neat retrieval system, select an ideal "safe place" immediately upon acquisition. Rats may live in rat's nests, but they can always find what they're looking for, being smarter than humans.

THE NOSE BUBBLE

We're living in a climate of pretentiousness unlike anything dreamed of in past history. If pretentiousness is a Satanic sin to be avoided, one must wonder if non-Satanists even recognize it when encountered. Like the sin of stupidity—how do you know if you sound or appear stupid to others who really *are* stupid? What I'm trying to get across is that certain Satanic sins are only sins when committed around other Satanists. Exaggerated pride is not laughable or counterproductive when in the company of those whose egos are already swollen beyond recognition. In fact, it is often the only means for survival.

It is no longer enough to be merely outstanding. If you are acknowledged as being special, you owe it to yourself (and others) to highlight your fame. You must put a frame around whatever you do. Elegancies have disappeared from the language due to vocabulary impoverishment. Instead of complaining about cultural decline, take advantage of it.

Learn double talk. It sounds impressive. And you can say absolutely nothing. Don't be self-conscious when you're speaking nonsense. People will respect you if your vocabulary is peppered with words they can't understand, even if they're not really words. Remember, pretentiousness pays off around stupes. A magician once said: "Always dress one step above your audience. If they are wearing jeans and shorts, wear a suit. If they're wearing suits, wear a tuxedo."

Don't tell someone that you're going to read them something you wrote. Say you are going to give a reading from your soon-to-be-published book. Get the idea? Put a big frame around it. If you don't say you're going to practice, they might care to listen. Say instead that you are selecting music for a film you are scoring and you would like their studied opinion. That way you'll have a captive audience who must actually listen to what you play. Interject what seem to be highly educated comments on structure, chording, phrasing, etc. Hit a handful of notes and ask what they think of that augmented flatted ninth—whether or not it fits the mood of the piece.

If you drive 10 miles to a shopping mall, say you are going out of town. If you are going back to school because summer vacation is over, say that you must resume your duties at the university.

When everyone's a big shot, you cannot be pretentious. People may hate you, but they will respect you.

If you don't care about respect, but want to be liked, show flaws. If another is ugly, stick a few warts on your face and sprinkle some fake dandruff in your hair. Everybody likes to feel superior. My favorite self-debaser is a nose bubble and a string of fake snot. I blow my nose with the bubble hidden in the tissue, slipping it into my nose. Removing the tissue, the bubble remains for all to see. I keep on talking like nothing is wrong, while my audience is deeply disturbed. After a couple of minutes, I pull out the tissue to blow my nose again. While faking a hearty blow, I shift the bubble to the other nostril, remove the tissue, and observe the dramatic results. I then lift the tissue back to my nose for an extra wipe, removing the bubble and inserting the long string of snot, which dangles down my lapel upon removal of the tissue. By this time, everyone is thoroughly disgusted, but they like me. They are better than me. They can tell everybody about Anton's snotty nose. It's better than reading the *Weekly World News,* because it actually happened to them!

Why I Can't Make Money

I've never been able to make money. It's a disease I have had to live with. I have had countless opportunities. I can't even ask for money. I've never learned the value of money because my goals have always been attainable without money. Goals such as love, romance, contentment, knowledge, capability, prestige, fame. I am so accustomed to getting all these things with little or no money, that when the time comes that I need to make money, I'm incompetent. If someone accuses me of "just being in it for the money," their lack of perception amuses me—and discloses their own personal failure and inability to succeed. They are saying, "I must pay dollars for whatever I get in life. You can't be any better than me, so you must pay for what you have in dollars, too." And then, in the next breath, "I only want to be appreciated for myself."

I have made billions of dollars—for others. I get satisfaction every time I see evidence of financial gain as a result of my machinations. Despite the most overt manifestations of financial gain directly attributable to me, I find it splendid that virtually no percentage, tithe, or emolument is proffered in gratitude to, or recognition of, me. This universal lack of reciprocity reaffirms my evaluation of the human race.

If I lack financial wealth, I have the next best thing: an appearance of it. For this, I am grateful, for it provides others a ready excuse to tip their lousy hands. Thus, they can say, "He doesn't need anything I would have to offer—he has more than enough already." Then, with a clear conscience, they can look the other way when it comes to giving the Devil his due. Besides, humans don't find Devils living on modest incomes very stimulating. The Prince of Darkness is surrounded by opulence. When He is petitioned, whether by Faust or Joe Blow, it is assumed that His priorities are the same as those His petitioner would desire. A fit and proper Devil, in order to tempt, must know well the cliched status symbols of common people—even those with lots of money.

It may be said that I was really inept at business and was suckered into projects that reaped no personal remuneration, that I sold myself too cheaply and was exploited. The fact is, I don't expect to make money. For that matter, I've never expected to do much of anything except maybe fart. I do things for people I like. If they make money, fine. I don't do things for people I don't like. Lord knows they would steal anything of mine they could—and have. But none escape.

It has been said that money can't buy love, but it can buy a good car to go looking for it. Money can't buy happiness, but it can buy an identity and stimulation—which even fools need. Money can't buy health, but it can provide enough financial security to keep you from worrying yourself sick. Money is good for most people to have. It can buy a TV, which is life itself to most. Whether you're rich or poor, it's good to have money. Personally, I dislike money, but the merchants I deal with insist upon it. As for bigger things: I don't need that kind of money. Certain persons do things for me, and I do things for them.

Don't Bathe

To Jules Goldschmidt

I never bathe. It is against my religious principles. Bathing is uncomfortable, messy, disruptive, and unhealthy. Bathing is like suicide. When life becomes more unbearable and uncomfortable than death, suicide is a worthy, practical, and gratifying alternative. When discomfort, stickiness, outside heat and itching become insurmountable, immersion in cool water is a blessing. If I am not uncomfortable when warm and dry, why should I change things?

If I stink in certain areas of my body, I wash those areas. I leave the rest alone. If I am not going to come into human contact, and can tolerate my own more pungent odors, I leave well enough alone. I don't wish to offend those for whom I care. Most others offend me more than I could ever return the favor, so why should I be charitable? If I can offend them in a manner even approaching how they offend me, more power to me.

Bathing is very unhealthy, in that it washes away natural enzymes and oils that significantly immunize the body from all manner of attack.

Bathing is unkind to other animals, in that it renders a human unpredictable and often unjustly untrustworthy. It creates confusion as to who is friend or foe. The only humans who need worry about such accurate evaluation are the untrustworthy and treacherous. Hence the worst people have good reason to bathe most often.

If one's diet is conducive to unsavory odor, because of ethnicity or preference, that person should live among others who share the same dietary resultants, rather than stink up an existing environment. That is nature's most basic means of stratification. One tribe smells different from another for good reason. Within the tribe, any deviation in normal odor is a sure sign that something is wrong with the stinker. Either he is ill, or guilty and has reason to fear his fellow tribesmen.

So you see, bathing and scent masking are dishonest. They provide a laudable means—in the guise of cleanliness (and goodness)—to conceal one's true nature and motivations. Anyone who deals with diversity in people, yet depends upon making a sale, must mask his scent.

The worst problem in bathing for scent masking is this: The indigenous odors—for better or worse—that are scrubbed away necessitate that the body's scent production work overtime to replenish whatever type of scent is habitual to the individual. Unlike perfumery, the process is reversed. Rather than cutting a stronger, objectionable animal scent, thus rendering it attractive, one's body naturally overcompensates by exaggeration. The result is that in a scrubbed and descented body, the very odor which offended is replenished even more pungently than ever!

Bathing is genetically disastrous and eugenically unsound. Through the fine art of scent masking, a woman who would be totally unsuited and unattractive to a desirable but unwise mate is able to breed and produce offspring of inferior genetic quality. Interestingly, this is an issue which is never explored, yet might yield frightening findings. Like telegony—though proven and applied in animal husbandry, it was long ago discarded as senseless quackery as applied to human animals, because it violated democratic ideas.

When creatures left the sea and walked on land, they still needed water inside them, being made up of vast percentages of fluid. Hence, they still must take on water internally in order to exist. Things are still the same. They rejected and left the habitat of water on the outside of their bodies to become man.

Love of the sea and attraction to water has nothing to do with a moral, societal, and psychological need to bathe. The only thing each has in common is water. I love the sea. I am invigorated by water, whether aerated or rushing, rippling or crashing. I like to live surrounded by water. I love the feel of crisp, cold water over my wrists and hands. As a child, I spent endless hours playing with boats in the cool water of a huge bathtub. I simply don't bathe, for some of the reasons I have given. To me, there is a difference between the feel of the salt spray while standing on the forecastle of a ship plunging through the sea; and the need to leap into a shower and wash away my own vital saltes, my identifying scent, and my unholy stinke. As far as I'm concerned, habitual bathing is for the pious, the frightened, the guilty, the idle, and the insecure.

THE ART OF INVISIBILITY

Very little that I know of has ever been written on the practical application of making oneself invisible. One excellent book by Steve Richards, *Invisibility,* tells the basic theory as studied by various disciplines, i.e. Cabalistic, Rosicrucian, etc. It provides esoteric exercises accordingly, but no real "tricks." Mystical, scientific, and magical principles notwithstanding, invisibility, like stage magic, is based on tricks. It tricks the brain into not seeing that which should be apparent. It is based on a simple premise, a law: "That which is present, should not be."

I have had a full-grown lion rattling the bars of his cage, not six feet away from a man who could not see him. The lion was in his quarters outside a kitchen, with a window in between. Heavy bars kept the lion from crashing through the window into the kitchen, should he wish to help prepare food, or dine at the table next to the window. One evening, after an informal seminar in another part of the building, everyone adjourned to the kitchen for coffee and refreshments. My lion, exuberant as a child at having lots of new company, tried to make his presence known by pawing at the bars of the window. One particularly scholarly-looking fellow was obliviously chatting away while holding his Styrofoam cup of coffee in one hand and a cookie in the other. Someone who found the lion's attempts to get attention amusing commented to the blasé fellow, "That lion is really something else, isn't he?" The guy just waved his cookie and kept talking. After another five minutes of holding forth, he looked in the direction of a particularly loud banging noise. He screamed at the top of his lungs, "THERE'S A LION OUT THERE!" His coffee, still quite hot, went all over the front of his suit and his cookie shot into the air.

The interesting thing was that he had been directly facing the lion's bid for attention all the time he stood talking. Others had seen and commented on the lion. To him, the lion was invisible. His mind was so organized, his intellect so preprogrammed, that the lion didn't exist. Lions are not in kitchens. One doesn't expect to encounter one there. Had the poor fellow gone through life waiting and hoping to walk into a kitchen and see a lion, matters might have been different.

Here's an example of the opposite: It is a blustery day on the new car lot. The flapping pennants are about the only visible movement. Five salesmen and one salesperson are standing around desperately waiting for a customer—any interested party—to step onto the lot. There are 85 new cars and vans that must be moved in the next two weeks. Oh boy! Here comes a prospect! A rumpled guy alights from his 10-year-old car, both very ordinary. The most outstanding thing about either is the message on the driver's t-shirt, but it is obscured by his zipper jacket.

Suddenly, he is center stage. All eyes are upon him. He is not about to perform a triple somersault from a trapeze only wander through the lot. He has 10 minutes until he picks up his wife from shopping at the mall. After a frantic allocation of sales personnel, it is determined that the Chosen One will approach him.

He is *not* invisible. At that moment, he is the most important man on earth. So great is the need to perceive a customer, that the salespeople would see a guy in a Brooks Brothers suit if a dog walked onto the lot and pissed on a tire. Unlike the Law of Invisibility, this is an example of high visibility based on expectation.

In Hollywood, tourists are celebrity conscious. The most minor actor will be spotted as he eats his pig-in-a-blankets at IHOP. The same performer would go unnoticed in Boise, Idaho—by the very family who spots him while on vacation in Hollywood. Expectation.

Conversely, Charles Bronson or Jimmy Carter could eat in a Fresno, Calif., McDonald's; and no one would suspect. Why? First of all, they would have aged or changed enough in appearance from what had been established. More importantly, "What would they be doing in a place like this?" even if a tiny bell should go off. In other words: it couldn't have been them, therefore it wasn't. Location is important to invisibility.

The tricks of invisibility are few. They must be flawlessly applied, however. If you want to be invisible, start by going where others, by their visual appearance, will have priority. Remember: People must want to see you, in order to maintain their acceptance of your reality. If you want them to notice you, give them brain candy. If not, give them an excuse to eliminate you from their view. A perfect example is how invisible you can become to a salesperson just before closing. If you have been neglected by a salesperson despite your attempts to catch his attention, chances are that by your appearance and demeanor, you would be better ignored. Professional thieves take advantage of this type of invisibility and walk out with anything they want. Their very presence is an annoyance, regardless of what they walk away with. This trick became so prevalent that exit checkers have become almost universal.

A quiet child will not be seen. They're expected to be noisy. Remove all expectations, and the person disappears. "Children should be seen and not heard" is a non sequitur. A child who is not heard will not be seen, and might as well be an accordion in a case.

Waiters and waitresses go unrecognized if they encounter a regular customer in a different location while wearing "civilian" clothes. If you present yourself the opposite of what others expect, they will miss you completely. As an exercise, start working your invisibility on people who have established expectations of you. Since invisibility is a visual phenomenon, you must properly alter your visual appearance.

Once you have mastered invisibility through visual alteration, you should start to practice invisibility through dislocation. That is simply being where you shouldn't be. It's surprising how outlandish one can appear, if he or she is in an environment devoid of deviation and no advance warnings are issued.

Timing is a valuable tool in invisibility. Not simply bad timing, but conflicting timing. Try going to a familiar place at a time when you would never be expected to appear, and observe how eyes that would normally register instant recognition sweep right over you.

There you have the principle ingredients of invisibility, employed individually or in combination, yet all dependent upon *expectation*. The three ingredients are *visual alteration, dislocation,* and *conflicting timing.* Without these simple tricks, the magician's stock in trade of "Now you see it, now you don't" could not exist. Personal invisibility is no more than another form of disappearance. Forget about your "visualization," "clouding," OOB exercises, etc. Instead, work on the aforementioned. You'll be amazed at the results.

The Details Make the Difference

Knowledge is not enough. It might be enough to set you apart from the rest, but not enough to bestow expertise. A sorcerer must be an expert in many things and be aware of subtleties and trivia that go beyond a superficial awareness. An example:

Someone mentions a scene in a Marx Brothers movie where Harpo appears smarter than he is presented. Someone else in the conversation remarks that Harpo was actually a very erudite fellow, and was a regular at the Algonquin Round Table. The rest of the group accepts that remark, for whatever it's supposed to confirm, and the conversation moves on.

Now, let's stratify the mental processes of three people present. The person at the top—the wizard—immediately knows details of the group mentioned at the Algonquin Hotel. The "average" listener is prepared to accept the statement, because he too has heard that Harpo traveled in intellectual circles, and may have even heard of the group in some context. Number three listener simply has been informed that Harpo was a smart guy. His mind has had little to retrieve.

The sorcerer not only knows about the group, but who was a part

141

of it, something of the other members, when the group was at its height, where the Algonquin Hotel was located, the physical appearance of the building and the effects its denizens had on the literary scene of that period.

The speaker may know of the group; that it was a sort of literary legend, but not be able to name its members. He may know that it flourished "in the old days" of New York, but may not know the exact location or appearance of the place—though he knows the relevance of the scene in the film he mentioned to Harpo's enhanced intellect. Hence his comment in the first place.

The third member of the trio, who may have memorized the kabbala and considers himself the most magical of the three, knows who Harpo is, as well as the other two Marx Brothers. (He doesn't know there were others.) He doesn't know what "erudition" means, but figures it must be something good, like having a lot of money. The Algonquin Hotel means nothing to him, let alone the "round table" except that he can relate it to Sir Arthur because when he was young he saw *Camelot.*

We have just seen a tangible example of automatic stratification. Each of the three minds has operated on a different frequency and processed the original comment differently.

If you are to consider yourself a sorcerer, you must be the most aware member of any group you enter. That means that you must be the wise man of the tribe, the shaman. Yet, you must never delude yourself that no one is mentally superior to yourself. If you do, you may be in for a rude awakening, leading to resentment on your part. Resentment means you are threatened, and whatever magical power you may have been able to exercise is diluted. If that becomes an occasional situation, the best way to deal with it is not to get even, but to get smart. Then you will move up a step towards a new level of stratification.

İnventi⊙ns

The greatest inventions are suppressed because they violate economic stability. If a new invention renders an established one obsolete, it will be resisted so long as there are vested interests in the old way. Progress and profit are incompatible. Profit has long been a greater incentive for the suppression of new ideas than it ever has been an incentive for development. There is more money to be made by stifling progress than by encouraging it. That is why inventions of revolutionary value are more often bought out by established interests.

Any revolutionary idea or invention will eventually surface "in due time"—meaning when it becomes so self-evident that an innovation is the only viable alternative to a long-impending dilemma. The rise of Satanism in the face of increased religious disillusionment is a glaring example.

There is seldom anything new—only reluctant acceptance of old inventions and principles which have been deliberately suppressed. Herd animals that people are, there will always be plenty of resistance against unorthodoxy.

The Dymaxion car of Buckminster Fuller and the Stout Scarab are of such historical importance that they cannot be overlooked. They are no longer an embarrassment because their inventors are dead and the inventions were doomed to rejection long enough for a "reinvention" process to be invoked by already-respected manufacturers. The personal luxury van has arrived.

I would like to add a "revolutionary room" to my house, wherein all manner of ridiculed but valid innovations reposed. Objects and furniture which may have had a short burst of tongue-in-cheek popularity would be displayed. What happened to the chair that one sat in backwards, resting on elbows and knees?

The only need for the internal combustion engine is that money is made on fuel.

"Perpetual motion" machines are a simple matter, using perpetual sources.

"Anti-gravity" is a term to misdirect from the incredible potential of existing gravity. The power of gravity, like solar power, is a means of energy without the expense or even the use of fuel. Both have been known and applied for a long time. What's holding things up?

Every wall in a building can be a storage wall. Why aren't they?

A functional and attractive home could be constructed by modular construction by the owner, with greater ease than a log cabin once was. Why isn't it being done?

Attractive and flattering clothing could be made and sold that would not go out of style, yet be durable and comfortable beyond anything now available. Why isn't it?

There should be no need for "collectibles" at inflated prices. Anything can be duplicated for personal or aesthetic reasons. All books and periodicals of the past can be microfiched and replicated. Why aren't they?

The reason: complacency, lack of imagination, and more than anything else, habit.

Humans will not do anything unless they are forced.

Someone has to force them. First, they must be afraid.

The only time an inventive idea will take hold is when it is forced.

Humans are not very strong in the discovery department.

The inventor, like the poet, is a dreamer. He invents because he must. He prefers to believe that his invention will make him a lot of money. In that way, he differs from the poet. He is victimized by thieves, if his invention is any good. At one time in this country, would-be inventors held the same high hopes as computerized writers now do. Most musicians now are composers. They invent. Just like Thomas Edison. Them and Edison. Birds of a feather. I feel a very inventive fart coming on.

THE WAY THINGS WERE

Every woman had a wet crotch. It was as anatomically natural as a moist mouth or damp nostrils. It was the way women were built. Different from men. They had an extra orifice. Men had an extra appendage. Simple as that. A man's sexual performance depended upon the efficiency of his penis. A woman's, on the condition of her vagina. Two sexes. Two distinctly different organs.

A woman who attempts to dry out her vaginal area is no different from a man who would bind or strangulate his penis.

If a woman had a distinctive odor which emanated from her vagina, it was meant to attract, not repel the opposite sex. That gem of wisdom was a part of the curriculum known as "the birds and the bees."

Some women had wetter crotches than others, depending on differences in body structure, emotional responses, etc. Some men had larger penises than others, as well. This was one of nature's inequities, despite the premise that all men are created equal. A woman whose crotch was wetter—or smellier—than most others was NOT stigmatized any more than was a more amply endowed man. Remember this. It is a valuable lesson.

Women did not wipe themselves dry after taking a pee, any more than a diner finishes his meal, wipes off his mouth and chin, then grasps and commences to wipe out the inside of his lips and gums.

As I recall, upon completion of urination, a woman usually hoisted her panties back up. A man replaced his penis back into his trousers. There was a poem common to the graffiti of all rest rooms that went, "No matter how much you shake or dance, the last few drops goes in your pants." Toilet paper was a convenience intended to clean one's arse, not scrub one's pussy. Of course, that was before women were taught to despise their own bodies. Can you imagine a rural house-wife tearing a page from the Sears catalog or using the corncob each time she peed?

Women, being constructed the way they were, and being permitted less self-discipline and rigidity than males, were excused if they suffered an episode of incontinence. They were considered errant if said episode occurred under conditions when and where it should have been avoided. This set of rules, being at best, subject to interpretation, is one of the things that contributed to a woman being "naughty," as opposed to the stalwart male mystique. Men could be "ribald" and even "coarse," but only a woman could be "naughty." Women were also allowed to be "fickle," "temperamental," and "emotional." That's why they could scream and cry without stigma.

Ladies' underwear was always yellowed in the crotch, unless freshly laundered. It contributed to the "Law of the Forbidden" because that particular liability engendered by woman's anatomical structure and toilet habits, might be surreptitiously discerned. Most women were, by today's standards, awful slobs. A favorite article of clothing (in impoverished circles, often the *only* one) would be worn day after day. Photo essays and ads in popular magazines gave the impression that women "laundered their dainty things" on a daily basis, when in harsh reality, it was joked that underpants were washed when they stuck to the wall when flung across the room.

A telling commentary on the foregoing was that every woman's first line of criticism towards an erstwhile friend was the horrid condition of the other's undergarments: "My God! Her underwear stands up by itself when she gets undressed!" Invariably, from my own observations, the informer was not without sin. It was not uncommon for a woman to wear *two* pairs of panties—one of thicker cotton to absorb the moisture for the outer, or more silken pair. The arrangement was nothing more than a sophisticated—though not always effective—substitute for diapers. The first time I encountered the phenomenon, I was nonplused, despite the puzzlement of my date about a strange excrescence over my chest. It seems I was recovering from a bad cold which had settled in my chest, and upon advice, had pinned a small towel under my shirt to keep my chest warm. My date (she later told me) thought I was concealing some sort of absorbed twin or tentacles under my shirt. It seems her own device of double underpants however, was common practice among women, with or without chest colds.

Πotes on Insomnia

Πature abhors a vacuum. I may have discovered a way to free my mind from inward-turning destructive thoughts. I usually have a song running through my head. It is a habit I take for granted. Perhaps it's saved me by preoccupying my mind with a tune, rather than abrasive input. Given my nature, I do my best to avoid outside influences. If I sing an imaginary song, it serves as a barrier. My brain cannot stand not to think, for better or worse. It cannot become "blank." Most intelligent people probably share this. Those who depend upon outside influences have readily empty heads. Their minds don't conjure up much of anything without a road map. That's why they seldom have insomnia. When there is no external stimulation, their minds are blank, and if tired enough, they easily fall asleep.

To an insomniac, thinking can be a curse. The brain is always in gear, hence sleep comes with difficulty. Counting sheep doesn't work because you don't REALLY care how many sheep there are. That's not something you might think about on your own. Hence, your brain won't accept it as a DISTRACTION. When you sing a song in your head, YOU choose it as a distraction. That's why it becomes omnipresent.

Playing a tune in your head is not enough to put you to sleep because it's already THERE. No conscious thought (remember, your brain must keep working, no matter what) can overcome the accursed vacuum. Neither does "planning" what you will contemplate as you try to sleep. It must be for real. Whatever it takes, it must be a genuine distraction which makes your mind push out all else.

Listening to banal TV or radio talk shows works for many, but there is a destructive toll. Your thoughts are still not your own, but those implanted subliminally by the TV or radio as it plays. You may be distracted enough to sleep, but you learn what someone else is teaching you. You subject yourself to a direct outside influence; one which preoccupies your brain enough to fill a dreaded vacuum, but of someone else's concern (and profit).

Here's how I do it: I take a simple keyboard and place it next to me in bed. I try different sounds (it's not necessary to be an audio engineer) until I hit upon one that can provide a noticeable, yet acceptable PRESENCE. I scan the keyboard and find a pitch that enhances the effect. I wad up a piece of paper or fold a matchbook and wedge it between the keys, so the note I want is held down, and sustained indefinitely.

I set the volume so the note is clearly audible, yet not obtrusive or abrasive. Just loud enough to be clearly heard, but not so loud that you can't wait for it to stop. This is very critical.

Lie down and relax and listen to the note. Associate whatever you can with that note: the throb of an engine, a generator, wind, surf, leaves rustling, etc. Commercially available sound effect generators work, but are limited in their range of frequencies, leaning heavily towards a "white noise" repertoire.

To test your pitch and volume level: As you lay there, the apparent volume should diminish significantly until it becomes a comfortable lull. Through trial and error, you should arrive at a pitch and volume that virtually anesthetizes you from the extraneous (and anxiety-producing) thoughts that normally prevent you from sleeping.

YOU have created your own optimum frequency to command

YOUR attention, and once enjoying the distraction provided, are rid of any harmful mental vacuum. Your mind has become favorably conditioned to a sound which you have "fooled" it into paying attention to and which it won't want to leave.

This principle is the same as "music to the ears" as applied to engine room sounds, traffic noises, etc.—whereby a thus comfortably conditioned listener thrust into still country air finds it unnerving.

I cannot overstress the importance of seeking and finding one's own personal frequency. The more discriminating the individual, the more finely tuned a compatible and effective distraction must be. "White noise" is not enough, though in itself, it anesthetizes. In its therapeutic application it lacks the volume and substance which provides any associative food for thought. If it is of consciously distracting volume—like a blow-hole or steam jet—it merely paralyses while frightening, rather than lulling one into a sleep state. The ideal balance is for a sound to be (a) personally arrived at, (b) pleasingly distracting, and (c) ambiguous enough to evoke imagery which necessitates that the brain think. A habitual "thinker" can *never* enjoy a vacuous mind. In the still of the night, the thinker's worst fears are magnified unless the stillness is broken and the mind is allowed to *construct* compatible thoughts. That's why the "customized" sound.

TOTAL ENVIRONMENTS:
SOME FURTHER SUGGESTIONS

Midway City
A Total Environment Community

The time is 1950. All lifestyle, aesthetics, and options of the period are permitted. The period embraced encompasses the first half of the 20th century, no later.

In 1950, one could still obtain and wear any clothing style of the past half-century, drive a vintage automobile, listen to and play music, live in a dwelling, learn about and discuss events, purchase consumer goods, effect values, or otherwise disport oneself in a manner indigenous to a fifty-year time span.

Castle Town
A Total Environment Community

The emphasis is on architectural style. Each dwelling is part of a complex consisting solely of castles, constructed on a scale conducive to practical living. There are no restrictions or dress codes; however, it is presumed each resident is antiquarian by predisposition. Buildings are in various castle forms; some Gothic, others Norman, in addition to Graustarkian, Fairy Tale, Scottish, Moorish, and other variations. The terrain is uneven, allowing for varying elevation of building sites. Some are in heavily wooded ravines and gullies, others upon rises. All are detached, except for specifically designed apartment and condominium units. Personal security, befitting the architecture, is encouraged by an abundance of walls, moats, and small windows. Clearly, this is not an enclave conducive to group activity.

Frontier Town
A Total Environment Community
Emphasis is on the Wild West and all its trappings. A strict dress code prevails. Motorized vehicles are banned except for those maintained for emergency use and otherwise kept out of sight. Knott's Berry Farm and Disneyland have operated similar enclaves, but as tourist attractions, for many years.

Other Themes
Old Russia, Montmartre Parisian, Old Heidelberg, New Napoli, New Espanola, etc., all with strict linguistic and dress requirements. Victorian and Edwardian England, with strict dialect and dress codes. American antebellum Deep South, with dialect and dress codes. Eskimo Iglooville. Neptune City (nautical architecture on dry land, with canals). Poseidonville (the same, except on real converted container vessels). Safari Land as full-time habitat. Outer Space (permanent *Flash Gordon/Star Trek/Star Wars* environment with rigidly enforced dress code). New Harlem, with strictly enforced dress and dialect codes. Renaissance Land. Prehistoria. Jesusburg, with enforced Biblical dress and preoccupation. Mosesburg (the same, only

Old Testament). Crime City, wherein everyone preys upon each other and weapons are openly vended. Boys' Town—a gay community with sidewalk measuring posts. Girls' Town (heavy on tattoo parlors, strict dress code with enforced baritone dialect, and beer served in dirty glasses). Xenophobia, with individual underground bunkers and isolation areas. Satan City, with emphasis on grotesque and bizarre architecture and landscaping, with appropriate dress requirements.

KEEPING BUSY
NOT KEEPING BUSY

Most people have developed the practice of indolence into a fine art. It is the closest they will ever come to perfecting a skill. As society increasingly encourages and rewards underachievers, incompetence becomes pragmatic. The uses of ineptitude are many, and sure to make life simpler, with less effort, than a display of aptitude.

A fine display of competence can be affected, however, while still maintaining one's ineptitude. Marvels of technology have provided awesome means by which a dolt may appear gifted. By these devices, brains and talent have become purchasable commodities, much easier to come by than anything else.

The supreme irony of all this is that it is easier for a naturally incompetent fool to purchase devices by which he might display great ability, than it is for a naturally gifted or accomplished person to acquire a proficiency in uselessness. It may take more effort and ability to be truly capable, but in order to present a convincing appearance of wit, wisdom, or ability, all it takes is the price of the right device.

If you are by nature industrious, you will feel guilty not "doing something worthwhile." Chances are, if you are that way, you have already accomplished more in life than you realize. It may be time to rest on your laurels. In our non-productive world, less is more. If you've put in your time, you should feel no guilt at performing useless tasks. Others perform them all the time, and have never even been useful for a brief period of their lives. Think of yourself as just making up for lost time.

A good habit to get into is an awareness that there are no disappointments in life—only relief. Playing the ineptitude game requires the ability to "get off the hook." Thus, accept any rejection or refusal as a means to avoid further responsibility. Rather than mope about, and feel insecure; rejoice that you have succeeded in eluding responsibility. Think of every act as a potential call to jury duty. Learn to rejoice at rejection.

When occasion dictates an appearance of activity on your part, go through motions. I don't mean "Go through the motions." It's not even necessary to adhere to certain expected movements. Any movement will do. Any kinetic accompaniment. You will be considered a great worker if you keep moving. Movement connotes effort. Without movement things seem effortless. If you can't move a lot, get your surroundings to move for you. Like a circus ringmaster, have lots of acts going on around you: a child chattering away, an animal jumping around, etc. Gesture occasionally.

Build a big frame around whatever you don't do. Your first impulse is to emphasize that which you actually do. It's easier to emphasize what you *don't* do. Utilize time spent by yourself to do nothing, while concocting elaborately furtive activities to reveal to others. Or better yet, simply allude to essential distractions. Excuse yourself when your laboratory calls, for there is much important work to be done.

Never apologize for neglecting another. Always present an image of an old-time floorwalker: "Ye-e-e-ess .... What can I do to help you? ... STOP BREATHING ON MY CARNATION!" Make others feel like the nuisances they probably are. The best way to *be* somebody is to *do* less.

Growing Up

I'm growing up now. The only alternative to growing up is growing old. How can I grow old gracefully? It's not the chronological passage of time that takes its toll nor demands extra attention. I don't worry about looking like an old fart. Probably it's because I never worried about not looking young. Youth and its exuberance never had any appeal, much less exerted any influence. How can one grow old, when one was never young?

Growing up has its advantages. Instead of complaining that you've wasted the best years of your life making unwise judgments and glaring errors, you rejoice that you've finally learned. "Too soon old and too late smart" need not apply. To remain a bit naive is to ensure not getting old. I have picked ways of remaining naive so that I won't have to worry about getting TOO smart. Hence, I can get smart in some ways—the ways that count—and remain ignorant about other things.

For example: I get smarter every day when it comes to humans and their motivations. I have a lifetime of retrospection from which to draw my comparisons and evaluations. If I begin to reevaluate people and events of my past, I see things I never before considered. I wouldn't make the same mistakes again. The wonderful thing about that is to see history repeating itself, but this time around being smart enough to say "No."

When I think about the amount of time I've wasted on subsequently worthless people and inconsequential causes, I abstain from most participation in parallel situations. After enough "learning" years, one can view almost every new situation as one parallel to an old one. That's why I will say, "No—I won't do that because it was lesson number fifty-eight."

As Thoreau observed, nothing really ever changes. Only the names, dates, and places. The situations remain the same. When you can understand and apply that principle, you have grown up. You refuse to waste your shortened time on games that have lost any appeal they might have had. Current events are seen as past events of little or no lasting consequence. In fact, the very predictability of current events frees one of concern over them, leaving one better prepared for life's genuine surprises. Surely, the only thing one can really be certain of is the unexpected.

All this is not to say that I regret anything. I consider each incident in my life, however painful, part of a learning experience—part of growing up.

I feel old most when I draw comparisons. Mostly economic comparisons. I suppose I'm bitter because an ice cream cone is no longer a nickel and you can't buy a home of your own for ten thousand dollars. If you don't get too old, there are compensations, though. Who needs an ice cream cone at any price, when virtual reality can put the same cold taste in your mouth. Who needs a real home, when you can design one of your personal liking and walk around in it—all with a convincing architectural program. Then, there is concern over the speed and capacity of one's present computer.

It is said that one of the attributes of the Nine Unknown Men is the faculty, knowing the power their knowledge confers, to remain aloof to the affairs of humans. I have seen firsthand how the media manipulates the masses, and how little truth ever gets out. The media serves to alleviate humans' boredom, not to inform. Returning to Thoreau: "Most people lead lives of quiet desperation."

Or at least they did. At a time when the illusion of one's own importance wasn't the sustaining factor that it is today, fifteen minutes of fame wasn't essential. In our present quest for immortality, there is little to be gained in leading a life of quiet desperation. The replacement is a life of frenetic complacency. The high noise levels and hyperkinetic pacing of media assault ensure that it will rub off on the viewer or listener, The resultant real-life pacing is fast. The faster people go through their activities (or rather, *appear* to go through their activities), the quicker they will dispose of obsolete consumer products. They are still doing what they are told—even more so, except with the illusion of independence. They no longer must shut up and say nothing. They can get on the internet and let the world know. Every man and woman has a voice. It matters little that the data from which they draw is limited to exactly just how much they should know.

Future Schlock

Ilook forward to the future to watch my son develop, and to remember. Nothing else. The future insofar as human events is concerned holds no attraction for me. Only more of the same as the present. This is not my world and as time progresses, the world is even farther removed from my own. I won't give examples. They are obvious to anyone who knows me.

The joy of the present is that the rest is past; and with that, being able to retrospectively evaluate. Each day I remain alive is another day to live in the past; to savor and relive the positive investments of my life, or to ruminate over and learn from my disappointments and mistakes. Whoever tries to rob me of the memories I have worked hard to accumulate and retain is my enemy. They take my greatest wealth. When I see the extent and quality of others' memories, I can understand why they begrudge me of mine.

What of the future? What does it hold? What can it possibly hold that is really worth looking forward to? Money? To use for what? A car I cannot drive, and have no place to store? Lavish meals I can't enjoy? A piece of furniture or theater organ or white grand piano that I have no room for? Books to read, when I have thousands already—many of which have yet to be read? People clamoring to meet me when I have little enough time for my own selfish interests? Travel to places

I have no desire or energy to visit, as a guest of someone who is of little or no interest to me? Applause and adulation at the cost of my own pacing and schedule? Experiencing events that necessitate trafficking with unstimulating, aesthetically ugly humans? Further success in areas which have already reaped enough? None of the above.

The future holds time. Each day provides me fresh opportunity to relive the past. I resist new shallow experience and useless awareness. It diminishes my memories. Don't bring me up to date. Then, I will have to process your contemporary garbage and neglect (or worse, dilute) my meaningful past.

The future holds technology—the miracles of innovation and production which can enhance my re-creation of the past. Research, development and production is thoughtlessly and compulsively paid for by drones and slaves. By-products become available that enable me to illicitly and secretly further my reconstructions. Slavish consumers make it economically possible for me to acquire new and useful tools.

Don't force me into the marketplace. I shun its denizens and their mindless pursuit of death. There is more pure stimulation in the use of this device upon which I write, than in all the passports and passage to foreign lands. When I contemplate the wonders of a computer chip, it rivals the building of the pyramids, and makes hollow the most lavish contemporary entertainment.

I derive greater stimulation and energy from sordid and cheap spectacles of the past than from the abysmal fake-desirability of the present. "Build for the future" is a meaningless phrase. It is a good answer to the question: "What do you do with all the money I promise you?"

Money spent in recreating and reclaiming the past is well spent. The greater the obsolescence, the less valuable the present and the more valuable the past. "Collectibles" abound when everything becomes obsolete. Today's obsolescence is tomorrow's collectible. I collect obsolete people and preserve them, then send them back into the world as collectibles. Then, when others say: "How interesting!"

I reply: "You too, could be interesting at some future date, if you could just allow yourself to go out of style. That's why you will never amount to anything as long as you live, and when you die, you will be no more than a fashionable corpse. By the time you might have become a collectible, your fashionable clothes will have rotted away. At least while you were alive, you could have prepared yourself for a tiny spark of immortality by studying and savoring the past."

As in all matters magical, "As above, so below" applies. IF the future is to hold anything, it will be to serve the conservators of the past. If I did not know and remember the past, present technology would provide no more than video games and surfing the internet. Don't think about the future. Then, if you're lucky, you might just experience it. With a little preliminary homework, you could even benefit from it.

GET A LIFE

As far as I'm concerned, I would like my organization, the Church of Satan, to exist as a cabal for the mutual endowment of those already occupied with interests and activities other than organizational. I have often stated that I like to think of the Church of Satan as an organization for non-joiners. Affiliation need not negate independence. Affiliation should be based on respect, rather than desperation. Respect for a set of principles and for other men and women who share those principles, yet who are not dependent on an organization to give substance to their lives. The obvious question arises: "Why then, would such persons need a Church of Satan?" The answer is, "They don't, unless it can do them some good." Affiliation should enhance one's life, rather than be a substitute for it.

Anyone who resists affiliation with the Church of Satan yet draws from it for any reason, personal or financial, is not independent, only parasitic. Accordingly, any vainglorious exemption from organizational affiliation, based on personal freedom and independence, falls upon deaf ears. That is scavenging of the lowest sort. It is the parasitic role of the groupie, the hanger-on, the lot louse, the kibitzer, the shnorrer, the cake eater, the panhandler who loiters outside a restaurant accosting diners as they depart. There is nothing admirable in hawking "independence" while sucking existence from a bloc of beneficially linked, but individually productive persons—in the present case, members of the Church of Satan. Translation: they want all the benefits of affiliation, with none of the responsibilities.

It will be argued that, Satanically speaking, if anyone can assume and maintain the aforementioned position of having one's cake and eating it too—more power to them. My answer to that one is: "Fine, but not with me or my outfit, they don't." And if anyone in my outfit supports such chicanery, they in turn, should quit the Church of Satan and start their own thing. Just don't expect to pull the same parasitic dodge yourself. It won't wash any better with you doing it. If your freedom stops at the end of my nose, your profit stops a whole lot further away than that.

Members of the Church of Satan may not be fulfilling their destinies to their complete satisfaction, but they do have destinies. The best of them have already taken steps to actualize those destinies. The Church Of Satan should serve as a generator for existing energy.

SATAN SPEAKS!

The stalest thing in the world is a timely joke that everyone's heard.

 ⌒〜

Those who are humorless should not be taken seriously. They take themselves so seriously, they leave no room for others to do likewise.

 ⌒〜

I never met a person who gave his profession as "comedian" who was witty.

 ⌒〜

Wit, like style, is not an acquired commodity. One either has it or does not.

$\odot$nly a fool mistakes laughter for humor and fashion for style.

Πy advice to whom someone says: "You must try MY [culinary specialty]": *Don't.*

Those who affect an appearance of poverty feel guilty about their affluence. Help them ease their consciences by taking advantage of them.

Those who spell "magic" with a "k" aren't.

Why am I a Satanist and not a "Wiccan" or "pagan"? I have found the so-called "occult community" so limited regarding anything of interest that I have little or no common denominators. My rejection of and disdain for occultniks is not based so much on ideological or philosophical grounds as it is on personal boredom. I simply cannot get enthused about their pet topics. I would rather hear Al Bowlley sing "Love is the Sweetest Thing" or Al Jolson belt out "Where Did Robinson Crusoe Go with Friday on a Saturday Night?" than discuss the historical nuances of Goddess worship. I'd prefer to read a book about unusual aircraft or forensic pathology instead of a treatise on crystal gazing. Please spare me your revelations that most well-adjusted Wiccans are real folks who pursue interests similar to mine—they don't. I haven't encountered one yet.

I have, however, met Satanists who share my interests. And can even discuss them. Plain and simple, I've found that Satanists are just more eclectic, worldly, and generally smarter. Since the First Great Cardinal Sin of Satanism is stupidity, I don't want to waste time on those whom I consider my inferiors. I believe that Wiccans and neo-pagans are a pretty dull-witted lot. Why else would they maintain their prevailing attitude toward Satanists, given the rational and reasonable explanations of contemporary Satanism available for the past quarter century? Can they read? Can they think beyond the "sexist" nude altars?

I foresee a breakthrough in cancer research wherein white sugar is both preventative and cure. My speculation is based on the vitriolic campaigns against sugar which are maintained by the masochistic and life-denying advocates of broccoli, brussels sprouts, raw cabbage, garlic, onions, and other such substances. Health food advocates are masochists. Most masochists secretly want to die. Cancer kills the concerned, masochistic or otherwise. Watch what masochists are eating, and eat the opposite. There are always more masochists than the world needs, as the vast majority of the population falls into that category. Therefore, they set the pace for the rest of humanity. They are the consumers who feed the coffers of greed. Theoretically, they are necessary. They are also the chumps, the suckers. Don't take their advice on anything, as everything in their lives is calculated to subjugate and contain them. Cancer researchers could have found a cure years ago, but the economy would have suffered badly. The masochists would have resisted the cure because they can never fully indulge themselves, except through denial.

Then there was the guy who moved to another town because he heard that most automobile accidents occur within a few blocks of where you live.

It's inaccurate to say that someone trembles all the time. Trembling is caused by unwanted movement intruding upon serenity at a steady but rapid rate of speed. Like discovering half a worm when eating an apple, one can only tremble *half* the time. The other half they are perfectly calm.

The reason you hear so many stories about how lawyers screw over their own clients is because to be taken, you must have something worth taking. A defendant would not hire a lawyer to defend him unless his interests were worth defending. As *all* lawyers in a civil case are looking out for their own best interests, the defendant becomes their primary source of gain. The claimant seeks to obtain what the defendant already has, and the defense is handsomely paid from what the defendant already has. Therefore, it behooves every defense attorney to *increase* his client's dilemma. In every civil suit the defendant cannot help but lose. Once a settlement has been awarded to a litigant, even without collusion, a defense attorney's first line of action is to convince his client that all is not lost. He can (for a fee) recoup some of his loss.

A comfortable falsehood will always win out over an uncomfortable truth.

The only person in recorded history to codify Satanism into an applicable religion is Anton Szandor LaVey.

If someone were to ask me what I considered the single most contributing factor to my personality, I would have to answer: "Avoidance of the influence of other people." This does not wholly imply independence, for I am certainly dependent upon others for many things. If I'm reclusive, it's because I don't want to subject myself to outside influences—for better or for worse. I want to draw as much as I can from my already established influences, be they experiential or contemplative. Any contact and interaction with others can color those influences, or worse yet, place them into conflict. Being basically agreeable, I recognize the dangers of social interaction, not to mention media exposure. It is easier to remove myself from them as much as possible.

One cannot be agreeable without running the risk of subjectivity. To be disagreeable is to be miserable, but often more objective. My idea of a contented life is to be neither an agreeable but susceptible fool, nor a miserable curmudgeon. When I interact with others, those are the resultant extremes, and I seem to live by extremes, like it or not. It will be suggested: "Why not balance things out? Why must you be one or the other? Try to be more adaptable." My answer is a question: "Why bother?" The loves of my life seem to be so removed from the vital stimulations of others, I want no part of a world outside of my own choosing.

When I say, "I am a very happy man in a compulsively unhappy world," It is because I clearly see that others wish to impose their masochistic needs upon me. It becomes a rejection of attempted conversion to a system I want no part of. So I slam the door on them, as though they were Jehovah's Witnesses.

I can't see what's so terrible about prison. It seems like a fine way to live. My only objection would be having to interact with the other inmates. No need to confront the outside world. Plenty of time to write and think. No transportation headaches—always a few steps from home. Medical and dental benefits. Regular meals of better quality than most on the outside. No clothing expenses. Free legal counsel. Mail privileges and free postage.

Daylight savings time is a useless relic of a Depression-era political device, like "a chicken in every pot," and the WPA. It mutates time in a manner that was calculated to provide wage slaves with an extra hour of beneficial sunshine after leaving their dreary daily jobs.

Now it is an annoyance, if only for reasons of inconvenience. In the past, most people had one watch, and one or two clocks. Clock faces displayed the time using two hands: minute and hour. Resetting twice a year was no project. Now, everything from VCRs to microwave cookers has a built-in clock with varying methods to set the time, displayed in a digital readout. That means you can't simply reset the hands on a watch or clock in a somewhat casual manner, but must synchronize several readouts to display identical time. This takes more time than ever, which is what advanced technology is supposed to save. Instead, you waste a lot of time resetting many clocks and watches.

Worse yet is the damage to your internal time clock, which cannot help but add to the rest of the problems that your worry-masters have induced. More clocks mean more reminders of what time it is. Reminders which establish and maintain a particular biorhythm into your life. This predictable pace is violated twice a year, throwing your timing completely off. Daylight saving time complicates, confuses and enslaves.

Modern jazz is nothing more than the Emperor's New Clothes. It is a group of tone-deaf, inept hopheads pretentiously playing at being musicians. The result sounds like they're playing different tunes simultaneously, each one out of tune.

It's a mistake for a shallow person to try to display another, more serious side of his or her nature. It invariably comes out so cliched and trite as to be laughable.

Many people who fall back on phrases like "more than words can say," "when words are not enough," or "beyond description," simply have limited vocabularies.

Until personal computers became popular, a mark of professional printing was that *both* margins were justified. A lot of training, skill, and "furniture," as well as expense went into a finished printed product. Now that justified margins are available to everyone, writers go out of their way to leave one margin ragged. I suppose, in keeping with the times, it looks more casual and laid back. To me, it looks like *poverty chic* pretentiousness and a lot messier.

One of the reasons I hate people so much is because they are basically an insecure, treacherous, dishonest lot. Gossip and soap opera are nothing more than a reflection of their daily lives: filled with sour grapes, nit-picking, belittling, and every manner of envy. No wonder those despicable traits have led to incurable greed. Whether on a grubby little get-something-for-nothing, win-the-lottery level, or on a corporate and political level, there is complete disregard for the lives of the most valuable fellow humans.

When there are too many soldiers, there can be no peace.
When there are too many doctors, there can be no health.
When there are too many lawyers, there can be no law.

The most legendary men and women share a secret past. As children, they were introverted, insecure, and shy. Despite parental support, they could never feel accepted into the activities of their young peers. These are truly the self-made men and women of the world. In a way, they were freaks as children, receiving encouragement at home, but finding only alienation outside. If they finished school, it was under tenuous conditions, even though they were much brighter and more gifted than their classmates. They were ridiculed as "nerds" and often were undersized or oversized in stature. "Awkward," "gawky," and other terms were used to describe them— but like the ugly duckling, once having established their identity, they eclipsed their peers. They were forced to forge their own identities, because no one else would do it for them—unless it was as an object of further ridicule.

The reason old acquaintances like to talk of how they "knew them when" is due to the flagrantly dramatic change which has been effected. Once tormentors become insecure, they will hasten to return a legend to his or her uneventful past at every opportunity. Where once the "average" could feel superior to the freak, it is their very "averageness" which later torments them. There is no one quite so judgmental as one who has known only mediocrity. An irony is that the same "knew him when" types are invariably fans of some other grouping's "freak"—one whom has never exhibited any pre-identity image to them in the first place. The James Deans and Marilyn Monroes of the world are idolized by fans who only know them by their self-made identities. That's why legends must discard past ties if they are to succeed. "Old friends" are not. They are disgruntled because their understated friend soared, while they stagnated. Family members who have led uneventful lives are often the worst offenders. They must content themselves with publishing Christmas family newsletters detailing Steve's (the "average" brother) important new job in marketing analysis, while the "oddball" of the same family is usually more important than anyone else they ever knew. Tribalism? An interesting paradox lies in that the very support once provided by parents can turn into resentment if an acquiescent offspring takes flight and attains independent fame.

Life constitutes conscious existence. There are many punishments worse than death. Death is negation of feeling, even to the least sensitive. Death is a cessation of conscious awareness. To one who has been insensitive while alive, death will come as no great blow.

A curse thrown against an enemy is many times more effective if death does not ensue. To the already-dead, death is small punishment. I curse my enemies into disrepute. Their identities are the only semblance of life they know and can feel; to be better than someone else their only goal. I make them feel worse than others. I give them disappointment and failure in their most commonplace endeavors. That is how I punish them. Disappointment, failure, and disrepute. They can only know rejection when I get through with them. To a herd animal, that is the most depressing and terrifying thing: to be denied the safety of the herd.

Inasmuch as most of my victims are already insecure, it is an easy matter to pull a few flimsy props out from under them and turn them into full-fledged laughingstock. In this manner, I destroy my enemies, and in a way which is a constant reminder of their sentence. There is not the blessing of permanent sleep and release from a painful existence; only increased torment. If they have high hopes, I give them disappointment. If they embark upon some small enterprise, I give them resounding failure. If their reputations have been held intact, I give them disrepute. If they strive for recognition, I give them ignominy. When someone says: "He died, you know," the response will be: "Oh ... you mean that fool?" The worst of all possible curses has taken effect. The memory of him must go though eternity being hit with a slap stick or rolled-up newspaper.

When standards of excellence are at their lowest, don't attempt to provide your best. It might be too good, and will be unappreciated, let alone recognized. Instead, provide something a little bit better than the woefully inferior, and you will be hailed as a great improvement.

The arbiters of quality, when confronted by a decision, are not so much inclined to ask: "How can we make a better product?" but to reassess: "Is it too good for them?"

A word of advice to collectors, conservators, pack rats, and hoarders: If you must store certain items, DON'T leave them with Other People. You will never, ever, see your things again. Always store them in a place of your own access.

There are four things one should never loan if you expect to get them back intact—if at all. They are your wife, your car, your gun, and your books.

If you loan money to a friend, forget it. You will lose both the money and the "friend."

What does it matter who wins in the parade of life, when the reviewing stand is filled with corpses.

When everyone is reading Nietzsche, I'll be watching Don Ameche.

Most people are such insensitive louts that the only things they respond to are Fear and Pain. If you want something done, give them potential consequences for *not* doing it—not rewards for doing it. Merchandising only succeeds when it provides pleasant solutions for dilemmas it creates. ("End worrisome____.") People fear consequences more than they entertain hope. If they go out of their way to invoke consequences (called "borrowing trouble"), they are masochists.

The public needs to be kept in fear. If there are not enough existing fears, more must be concocted. The premise is that everybody is afraid of something. Discover that fear, play upon it, and enslave.

In a world of questionable identities, loss of identity equates to fear of rejection. Among herd animals, being banished from the herd is disastrous. Man is by his proven nature a herd animal. The price of nonconformity has always been high.

Understandably, those who espouse "freedom from fear" the most are those who provide a convenient enemy—one who must be vanquished and is ravening to take away their freedom. There can be no "freedom" unless some tyranny is provided to defend *against*. That's why villains are in constant demand.

The world is NOT a stage upon which we are all actors playing a part. In this world, there are the performers and there is the audience. They are never interchangeable. The members of the audience are the followers. The performers are the leaders. If a person is one, there is no chance that he can become the other.

W̲hen an entire society is a small group, it is called a cult. When a cult grows big enough, it is called a society. Both are rigidly conformist. The first requirement of either a cult or a society is obedience to its rules, conformity to its principles.

❧

D̲o not mistakenly think that selective breeding is a thing of the future. It has been with us for at least two generations. What is not realized is that the State makes the selection for you. The only reason for the encouragement of race-mixing is not one of equality or idealism. It is to ultimately create a global village of like-minded people who all respond to the same inducements. The old joke about selling ice boxes to Eskimos loses its meaning if Eskimos buy as many ice boxes as Fiji Islanders. Cultural differences must only exist in self-conscious studies, not in actuality. In actuality, an emphasis must be placed upon cultural homogenization, and whatever selective breeding contributes to it. It is harmless to the State if you *study* ethnic diversity, so long as you don't practice it.

Diversity is the enemy of herd mentality. Using a veneer of integration and brotherhood, the State insures that all humans are motivated by the same priorities. What an Asian wants, is what a Latino wants, is what an Anglo wants, is what a Native American and African American ... *all* want. As seen on TV. In other words; talk about your roots, dwell upon your heritage, study your ancestry, but *live* like everybody else. That, in turn, translates to: buy the same products, discard them at the appointed time, and then buy new ones.

Altogether, a sweet arrangement by the State: encouragement to flaunt one's ethnicity, while all the while responding to universal consumer dictates.

There is but a single purpose in the present form of selective breeding. More new people means more new customers. That's why a bonus is paid for having more children. Why settle for a limited market? A global village equals a global market.

∾

Animals think it is very funny to watch humans fucking, because no matter how hard they try, the humans cannot seem to find a comfortable position.

∾

"God takes care of drunks and fools" is inaccurate. In truth, he doesn't even notice them. That's why nothing bad happens to them. I proceed on an assumption that God is an asshole, and only notices those who don't deserve his dubious "attention": the sensitive, the just, the capable, the talented, the gifted. They are the butterflies whom God pulls the wings off of. You must be something special to be cursed by God. That is why I give my respect to Satan.

∾

Life is for the living. Death, too, is for the living. If you are fascinated or entertained by death, make the most of it while you're alive. When you really are dead, it won't hold any interest at all.

∾

Never let it be said that I gave my life for any cause, but rather that I took advantage of my impending death.

İ would rather see my enemies live to regret their words and deeds against me, than for them to die a horrible death. If they were not insecure, they could not have been so indiscreet as to attack me. Clearly, they are either stupid or nurturing a masochistic death wish. If they are stupid, they will blunder themselves into fresh dilemmas, which will exacerbate their feelings of worthlessness. If they seek the ultimate form of negative reinforcement, I don't wish to bless them for their attacks upon me. Better, they should go through life bearing even greater pain than when they provoked me. Then, they are truly between the horns of an intensified dilemma. By their very nature, they cannot make things right with me, once they regret their indiscretion. Nor can they obtain the satisfaction of death at my hands. I have sentenced them: not for life, but to life. Their jailers are their regrets, and they are brutal.